# EMERGE MINDFULLY

Less Stress and More Joy from Difficult Times

## MICHEL E. SPRUANCE

**BALBOA.**PRESS
A DIVISION OF HAY HOUSE

Balboa Press books may be ordered through booksellers or by contacting:

Balboa Press
A Division of Hay House
1663 Liberty Drive
Bloomington, IN 47403
www.balboapress.com
844-682-1282

Because of the dynamic nature of the Internet, any web addresses or links contained in this book may have changed since publication and may no longer be valid. The views expressed in this work are solely those of the author and do not necessarily reflect the views of the publisher, and the publisher hereby disclaims any responsibility for them.

The author of this book does not dispense medical advice or prescribe the use of any technique as a form of treatment for physical, emotional, or medical problems without the advice of a physician, either directly or indirectly. The intent of the author is only to offer information of a general nature to help you in your quest for emotional and spiritual well-being. In the event you use any of the information in this book for yourself, which is your constitutional right, the author and the publisher assume no responsibility for your actions.

Any people depicted in stock imagery provided by Getty Images are models, and such images are being used for illustrative purposes only.
Certain stock imagery © Getty Images.

Print information available on the last page.

ISBN: 978-1-9822-7797-0 (sc)
ISBN: 978-1-9822-7799-4 (hc)
ISBN: 978-1-9822-7798-7 (e)

Library of Congress Control Number: 2021924849

Balboa Press rev. date: 03/18/2022

This book is dedicated to my family. You are my constant teachers day in and day out. I strive to live this work because I love you. Thank you for your incredible love and support. And to the ancestors and teachers who came before me: thank you for lighting the way.

# CONTENTS

# INTRODUCTION

This book is a love letter to the world. What I want for you, for me, for our world, is that we can live into our potential as kind, brilliant, loving beings. I feel moved to share this curated set of mindfulness tools that I believe can uplift us to build a world we want, rather than return to a world that was.

Everything in this book is an offering from my heart and my own experience. As I strive to live mindfulness each day, I learn, I grow, and I stretch. I am on this journey with you, and I use every single tool in this book in my own life—sometimes well, sometimes poorly.

I offer these tools because they work. With practice over time, my life becomes more joyful and less difficult. And sometimes, in a moment, these tools can shift me from despair, fear, and sadness to deep, deep delight and peace.

On that note, I invite you on this journey of emerging with me, creating a new world for yourself moment by moment, piece by piece.

# WELCOME TO YOUR MINDFUL REENTRY

## WHY THIS BOOK? WHY NOW?

You deserve to live a fulfilled and joyful life. It doesn't mean that it is always straightforward or simple, and it certainly doesn't mean you won't experience difficulty and hardship. A fulfilled and joyful life includes traveling through dark winters as well as bright summers, and all of the transitions in between.

When you nurture yourself with kindness through your winters of difficulty, chaos, uncertainty, or despair, you renew yourself and step back into the world stronger and more alive than before.

If you've picked up this book, some part of you is calling to be nurtured into something new. Perhaps you found this book while recovering from the COVID-19 pandemic, or perhaps you found it while in a life transition such as a job change or divorce. Perhaps you are experiencing what feels like your own very dark time, and this book appeared, and you aren't even sure why exactly.

And yet, something in you is stirring. You sense spring will follow winter, and you are curious about how to reemerge in a way that feels authentically alive and less at the whim of the world. Eyeing a new reality, you tiptoe back into the world, and this book is meant to help you emerge from difficult times into a new, healthy normal that *you choose*.

Throughout this book, I'll reference the pandemic of 2020–2021 as a shared experience. You can apply all of these lessons to your personal transitions or challenges. No matter your personal story, the practices in this book will help you imagine living vibrantly, giving you practical tools to have less stress and more joy as you build your life on your terms.

What is interesting about referencing the pandemic of 2020–2021 is that it has been a shared global experience. Over time, we are emerging into our old world, and that world is not the same world we had left. And this process is cyclical, providing the perfect example of how to emerge into the life you want from any difficult or uncertain time.

As we find our way forward from the pandemic, I've spoken to so many folks who are scared in one way or the other. "What if this happens again? Can I trust the vaccine? Can I trust the people who don't take the vaccine? What if my company never goes back to the office? What if my company tells me I have to go back before I'm ready? What does all this mean for schools? Will my business survive next year? I don't want to go back to the way it was before." Most folks are exhausted.

And the rules are still shifting, just as they have been since March of 2020. All of that uncertainty causes stress. I'm not talking vaguely about stress here. I'm talking about the real physiological fight-or-flight reaction that is constantly triggered in your nervous system as you try to navigate these perpetually changing waters.

And here is the thing: even if you are reading this years past the pandemic, when you are in your own difficult winter or challenging transition, it feels just like all of what I described above. Often you will not know who to trust or what to trust. You'll lose sleep and feel isolated. You'll exhaust yourself. This is how stress occurs. This is the human condition.

Because the human condition is timeless, the practices in this book are timeless, and they offer an effective antidote to the stress response. Here you'll be given simple tools you can use to clear the stress out of your nervous system instantly. You'll enjoy exercises created to help you step back into your life so that it feels like *you are choosing* your life rather than just surviving it.

I'm not promising unicorns and rainbows, although rainbows are always a possibility. I do promise that if you try the strategies in this book, you'll very likely sleep better, be happier, and make more life-affirming choices as you navigate the continued flux of our world. These are timeless and proven strategies packaged to make a difference for you right now.

You deserve to define what reemerging into a new world looks like. You need not be at the whim of fear, reactions, and anxiety. You can make healthy choices to stay grounded and move into the world intentionally, in a way that nourishes both you and your community.

# WHAT'S HERE TO SUPPORT YOU?

I own a yoga studio in downtown Seattle, right in the heart of what has been the deserted land of Amazon employees since March 1, 2020. As my employees and I have worked to keep this small business afloat, we've noticed that things have seemed to shift about every three weeks. Three weeks also seems to be a timeframe that folks feel they can commit to without being overwhelmed.

Thus, I've designed this book as a three-week deep dive into reclaiming your life. The beauty here is that the book is short enough to work through in this three-week cycle. Then, likely by the time you get through the book, something new will have shifted, and you can return to the exercises that will serve you again.

In that way, this work is perennial. While you embrace the reality of right now—emerging two steps forward and one step back from our shared experience of COVID-19—the book provides applicable tools you can reference again and again. And I hope you will.

Learning to live mindfully is a circuitous path. My own journey to embody mindfulness as a mom, business owner, wife, and more looks much like our emergence from the pandemic. I have two wins where I handle the stress with my three-year-old brilliantly and then encounter a giant fail the next time.

While the exercises and information in this book build on each other, you can also skip around in the text. If something catches your eye, pause and notice if it's right for you (more on how to do that later). Here, you get to listen deeply to your inner wisdom about what is healthy and right for you right now. No one else can tell you that, even as we collectively do our part to build our world anew.

Each week you'll encounter a different theme to help you create a purposeful and nourishing reentry into the world. Along that theme, you'll find tools, practices, and assignments to help you stop reacting to the world and get you into the driver's seat to create your new, healthy normal.

Each week consists of five discrete elements:

1. *On The Go Mindfulness*: anytime, anywhere mindfulness tools to help you feel grounded and grateful as you move through daily life

2. *Daily Meditation:* 5-minute daily meditation practices offer you a moment to pause, breathe, and develop your mindfulness muscle

3. *Daily de-stress practices*: quick, easy ways to move stress out of your nervous system

4. *Lessons*: applied mindfulness lessons to help you define what matters most to you, set healthy boundaries, and more

5. *Well-being practice*: a short exercise that will cultivate your ongoing well-being

# Get the Most from This Book

**Do just what you need, and let go of thinking you have to do it all.** I'll make some suggestions below about what to use when. I'm offering you tools you can use as you need them. They are written here in this three-week crash course to get you moving, and you can select any one or two in a week that work for you.

**Skim each week before you launch, and choose the tools you'll commit to.** Once you skim the week, you can pause and sense which tools you need for the week. At the beginning of the week, I offer a suggestion about which things to select, and you can chart your own path, of course.

As a general rule, I encourage you to do the following each week:

- Select either the on-the-go mindfulness or the formal daily meditation practice and commit to it. If you feel up to it, you can integrate both, and starting with one is perfect.
- Skim and try the daily de-stress practice for the week and become familiar with it. Then if you need to shake some stress free, you'll have a tool to do so. These practices build on each other, and you could just keep using the practices from week one if you like.

- Implement the lessons from the week, such as "Knowing What You Want" or "Breaking Free from Reactions." Set aside twenty minutes to read and do each lesson during your week. That's a total of forty minutes, as there are two lessons in each week. I recommend you put those toward the front of your week if you can. And don't stress it if you can't.
- If you still have bandwidth and want more, enjoy the "Cultivate Well-Being" section in each week. Maybe right now it's more than you need. You choose.
- Take ten minutes at the end of each week to pause and reflect on how the tools worked for you and choose how you want to move forward. That's all.

**Commit to one mindfulness practice each week.** This commitment is huge in giving you back a sense of choice in your life. If you don't get to your mindfulness practice one day, don't worry. Start again the next day. Be light with it *and* committed to it. Growing your mindfulness muscle will change your life. (More on that in the next section.)

**Prepare your on-the-spot de-stress tools as you read them.** What do I mean by that? As you read about the daily de-stress tools, have some sticky notes handy to write them on, or put a reminder in your phone. Then you'll have these tools ready for you when you need them during the week. As I said, just skim the sections and try them quickly. You'll see what I mean.

**Make this work for you.** This book is not another thing to stress out about. I can guarantee that if you use these tools you'll feel better about your reentry into the world and happier overall. My goal is to give you back a sense of power and choice in your life. That means you get to choose which tools you use and when to use them. So, if you want to jump around in the book, jump around. If you want to follow the recipe set out here, do that. If you want to take six weeks instead of three, do that. Trust that if you are working mindfully you'll know what to do when.

**Let me guide you.** Some of the practices in this book are just nicer when someone guides you. This entire book exists as a video e-course. You can find a link in the back of the book with a discount code to access the full course.

# An Introduction to Mindfulness

"*Look past your thoughts, so you may drink the pure nectar of This Moment.*"—Rumi

Mindfulness is a cornerstone of this program because it is an effective tool to help you move beyond your thoughts and worries to the place where gratitude, joy, peace, and intentional action live within you.

Mindfulness can be defined as *paying attention on purpose to the present moment with kindness and curiosity.*

Sounds simple. It is simple, and it is a muscle that takes some time for us to build. Many of us were not taught how to pay attention to the present moment, let alone to meet that moment with curiosity and kindness. In fact, many of us were taught from a young age that we should be planning, strategizing, organizing, and evaluating at every moment.

Let's examine this a little more. To be mindful, the first step is to actually notice what is what going on, either internally, externally, or both. That can mean noticing how your body feels, the emotions that are present, or the thoughts you are thinking. It can also mean noticing what is occurring around you, everything from the buds on the trees, to the sounds in the distance, to seeing and hearing the person who is speaking to you. Your awareness is 100% with whatever is occurring, moment by moment.

Truly being 100% present to what is, in any given moment, is a win by any standard. And it is not just the fact of paying attention that matters, but *how* you pay attention that matters. In the definition of mindfulness I've offered above, paying attention with kindness and curiosity is paramount to the experience of mindfulness.

These two ingredients, kindness and curiosity, are really the lynchpin. Many of us can pay attention, only to turn on ourselves with judgement. Let's face it, some of us are just downright mean to ourselves when we pause to notice our thoughts, actions, and experiences. The Oxford dictionary offers that kindness is the quality of being friendly, generous, and considerate. Imagine simply watching yourself and those around you with a friendly, generous, and considerate outlook. That is a far cry from the kind of mental whipping many of us dish up as we move through our days.

Paying attention with curiosity brings yet another dimension to mindfulness. To be curious about the present moment is to be interested in what is going on. Instead of imagining that I already know everything about what is happening, curiosity opens my awareness and allows me to investigate. I can question, "is this really what I think?" "What is that sensation in my belly telling me?" Curiosity in this way opens the door to new seeing, new options, and sometimes, simply more ease with the world as it is. This kind of curiosity can also nurture kindness and friendliness.

So *why* practice this particular way of paying attention? The benefits of mindfulness are vast, and I'm going to stick to the three main reasons why it is an essential tool in keeping you moving toward a healthy, empowered life:

- Mindfulness balances your nervous system
- Mindfulness can curb rumination
- Mindfulness connects you to your body sensations

One reason mindfulness is so effective for your reentry is that it helps balance your nervous system, calming the part of your nervous system that initiates the fight-or-flight response (your sympathetic nervous system). As you ease the fight-or-flight response, you gain access to a myriad of choices you simply don't have when you are under stress.

When I'm stressed, I make notoriously bad decisions, such as eating the whole pint of ice cream, having another glass of wine, not exercising, or snapping at the people I love the most. Anything in there sound familiar? Perhaps you have a special brand of stress-induced self-sabotage.

Are you aware of your self-sabotage? And, if you are, do you notice guilt or discomfort as you bring it to mind? I certainly feel yucky when I see my self-sabotage clearly. Yet clearly seeing my patterns is the very thing that can free me—and you. When we bring mindful attention with curiosity and kindness toward our stress and its secondary behaviors, the angst loosens and we get to choose our way intentionally.

And the more you practice mindfulness, you sidestep the self-sabotage in the first place. As you learn to notice stress arise in your body, you can use the tools of mindfulness to clear it out before it takes over.

Mindfulness also curbs rumination, some of the thinking patterns that underlie anxiety and depression. As rumination subsides, you may even notice gratitude, simple pleasures, and more loving kindness in its place.

One of my clients noted how implementing two of on-the-go mindfulness tools helped her shift instantly from stress and fear to gratitude throughout her day. And it's the same for me. The other day I was all caught up with thinking about negotiating a new lease for my yoga studio while I was in the shower.

In a flash I realized what I was doing. I paused and held the soap to my nose, taking in a deep breath. The smell of lemon verbena made me smile. I felt the stress drain out of my body and I committed to staying 100 percent present for the rest of my shower (without worries about my landlord joining me). When it was time to sit down and actually do something with the lease, it turned out the only thing to be done right then was a pretty simple communication. Certainly not worth letting it take over my shower, or sleep, or relationships, or any other part of my life.

Lastly, mindfulness practices offer you the most direct connection to your body's sensations—a barometer for your well-being. Your body sensations tell you what you need and what is healthy for you, often faster than your thinking mind can compute. You'll learn to harness this tool throughout this book.

To be honest, if you get one thing from this book—listening to your body's cues—you will be light-years ahead in building a fulfilling, happy life. Honing your ability to feel your body speaking to you, especially the subtle sensations of stress arising, can change the way you navigate your whole life. It certainly has changed mine. I use my body's sensations to help me make choices everywhere from how to work with a screaming three-year-old, to who to hire at my business, to this lease I've been referencing.

## How Do You Do This Mindfulness Thing? What If You've Already Tried It and Failed?

I invite you to get curious with your experience of mindfulness. I know from experience that mindfulness is doable and worth it, even for the biggest skeptics. Over the twenty years I've been on my mindfulness journey, I can promise that I've never once wished I hadn't used it. On the contrary, my lifelong goal is to learn to live my whole life this way, not because I should, but because it feels good. I have watched the practice bring relief, ease, and joy to many in times of sadness, pain, and uncertainty. It can work for you too.

Having said that, it's likely that some of you have already tried mindfulness and felt like it just wasn't working or worth doing. While mindfulness is simple, most of us were not taught this skill from a young age. Our brains are not wired to pay attention to the present moment with curiosity and kindness. We need to patiently build the muscle, just like lifting weights at the gym.

We also have a cultural misnomer that mindfulness means clearing your mind, stopping your thoughts, or feeling peaceful. Sometimes those things happen when you practice being mindful, but not always. Most likely, thoughts will come and go. Sometimes they will be quite persistent. Sometimes you'll travel to the past. Sometimes you'll compose an email in your head. And sometimes you'll have comfortable and uncomfortable body sensations. You might hear music. You might hear silence. It's all expected and perfect.

Here are some guiding principles that will help make your mindfulness practice accessible and enjoyable:

- **Be kind.** First take out the "should." You do not *need* to do this. You are already perfect just as you are. Next know that you are not supposed to be good at being mindful. Mindfulness practices are opportunities to be kind with yourself and the process.

- **Let thoughts be thoughts.** Nope, you are not supposed to stop thinking. Instead, you get to start noticing that you have thoughts. Take that in. You get to notice that you *have* thoughts, and sometimes what you see in that process is that you are not your thoughts. That's all. Just witness the thoughts. Sometimes they will quiet down. Sometimes they will race. It is all good.

- **You are training a puppy.** Think of this whole process, and especially your mind, as a really cute little puppy. For real—picture your mind as a puppy. What color is it? What's its name? What size is it? What's your favorite thing about this puppy? Now it's a puppy right? So it jumps on your clean pants with muddy paws. It pees everywhere. You get annoyed, but really, what the puppy needs to succeed is a lot of patience, love, and redirecting. That's pretty much your mind.

- **Failure is growth.** You are going to get lost in trains of thought, especially when you are newer to this. Every time you notice this and come back to the anchor you are trying to pay attention to, *you win*! It's like you've lifted a new personal best at the gym.

With these guiding principles, mindfulness can be kind, light, and joyful. This is not another thing to beat yourself up over. You are wiring new synaptic connections in your brain. That's really cool work. Enjoy the journey.

# Week 1:

# TAKE THE REINS

---

Welcome to week 1 when you take back the reins of your life. This is the week when you start to feel like you make choices for your life from what you want, rather than from reaction and fear.

There is a lot in life you cannot control. This has always been true, and right now, more of us feel this truth more viscerally than we used to.

This is good news.

"Really?" you ask.

Really. A lot of good is possible in all of us having the communal rug pulled out from under us. So many folks I work with have reflected that they don't really want life to go back to exactly the way it was. They've started to see clearly what wasn't working in their personal lives and in the broader community. From too much work travel, to too much stuff in their homes, onward to bigger issues of racism and an underlying decay of democracy, so many of us don't want to go backward. We want to go forward.

I honor and recognize that living through this pandemic has been difficult for all of us, and for some, it has been painful beyond anything else they have experienced before. We have individually and collectively held a great deal of loss and grief in many aspects of our lives.

You may have also been asked to do many new and often uncomfortable things at the same time, such as working from your coffee table with roommates at the dining table, or schooling at home while holding down your full-time job, or moving your parents internationally after losing family to COVID-19, or feeling awkward about asking your colleagues to keep their masks on.

The very structures that held our lives in place were shaken. If you allow it, this process can be a profound opportunity to bring into view what matters most in your life. This is the clear vision I'm speaking to, and it is a foundation for building your new and healthy normal.

It can begin with the personal. I've heard many of my clients question the lives they had been living. Why were they flying every week to a new location for work, sometimes to three different cities in five days? Why were they commuting 1½ hours each way? Why hadn't they gone on that vacation? Why hadn't they spent more time with their parents?

One particularly vivid comment came from a friend who said, "What am I going to do with all these shoes in my closet?" She looked in the Zoom box, stunned with herself. She couldn't imagine how she had amassed so many shoes in her lifetime considering she had spent the last months barefoot, in slippers, or in running shoes.

We've also come to new levels of collective clear sight. In the United States—and, in many ways, around the world—deep political divides have come into stark view. Institutionalized racial injustice is coming into focus for many white folks in the US for the first time. Fires, snowstorms, hurricanes, and tornadoes have grown in intensity, requiring us to see the devastation before us. We have the choice to tackle and heal these complex issues if we can turn toward ourselves and each other with kindness and curiosity.

> Wow—put all in one place, that is a lot. In fact, now is the perfect time to pause, close your eyes, and take a breath. You might even want to put your hands on your heart. Notice your physical sensations and your emotions. After a few breaths, open your eyes and continue on, taking one last long exhale out of your mouth.

Reading all of that so plainly can feel like a lot. And yet, without this kind of honesty, these forces leave you powerless and choiceless. A cornerstone of your mindful reentry is choosing your life, rather than being at the whim of the world.

Many of us have been taught that we are supposed to control our lives, often by tamping down our emotions and unsavory thoughts. This week, your mindful reentry will help you learn to hold your honest experiences with curiosity and kindness so that you get to choose a healthy sense of what you can control, specifically with a focus on your well-being and how *you* want to approach your reentry into the world.

*Instead of living through this like a terrified novice on a runaway horse, you get to take the reins, slow the horse, and decide what direction to go and how you want that to feel.* This week you will take those reins. You'll define what you want in your life, break free from reactions that keep you in negative cycles, and develop tools to move into the world with a sense of inner calm and power.

This week, I encourage you to skim the entire week. Next, choose one mindfulness practice to commit to for the week. Make space to do lessons 1 and 2, and check out the daily de-stress in case you need it along the way. If you want more, do more! If this is too much, adjust as necessary. *You get to choose.*

# On-the-Go Mindfulness

## Mindfulness in Everyday Activities

*"While washing the dishes one should only be washing the dishes, which means that while washing the dishes one should be completely aware of the fact that one is washing the dishes ... The fact that I am standing there and washing these bowls is a wondrous reality. I'm being completely myself, following my breath, conscious of my presence, and conscious of my thoughts and actions. There is no way I can be tossed around mindlessly like a bottle slapped here and there on the waves."—Thich Nhat Hanh*

By choosing your now, you choose your future. One of the things that mindfulness gives you are moments when you are actually in the present moment. This sounds so silly, I know. It seems like, "Of course I'm here in this present moment."

If you think about it though, how often are you 100 percent fully experiencing the actual moment without thinking about something else? If you are like the majority of folks I know, you likely spend your time brushing your teeth while thinking about your morning to-do list or all the things you need to do before you get the kids in the car. Or, perhaps while you grab some coffee and drink it as you walk out your door, you're composing an email to your boss.

Here is the thing: life comes to us moment by moment. The only place where you have real choices in your life are in each of these little moments—not someday, and certainly not in the past.

What happens, though, is that we spend the majority of our moments planning for a future (wishing we could make choices and hoping we'll be able to make those choices) or retelling ourselves about a past (usually time spent here is not the happy past either).

*The only place where you can choose your future is the present moment— the moment you are living right now.* Right now you can pause and see clearly. Right now you can attend to what you need. Right now you can make a choice that will create your future.

This is where I get excited about sharing on-the-go mindfulness because it is something you can do as life comes at you, moment by moment. Something new arises—new guidelines from the CDC, a new workplace initiative, an unexpected health complication—any of this will throw your nervous system into the fight-or-flight response and you will lose your ability to choose your way. With a quick on-the-go mindfulness intervention, you set your nervous system right and reconnect to your executive thinking. Choice comes back online, and you are able to move forward, sometimes in just seconds.

## THE PRACTICES

These mini mindfulness practices are a great way to dip your toe in the water of mindfulness, relieve some stress, and refresh your mind and your mood. They can be fun and light, especially as you bring curiosity and kindness to the process.

On-the-go mindfulness is made up of two quick and simple parts:

1. An activity you already do in the day becomes a quick mindfulness practice
2. At the end, *stop* for one breath and notice how you feel overall

STOP is an acronym offered by the UCLA Mindful Awareness Research Center, meaning:

**S.** Stop

**T.** Take a breath

**O.** Observe

**P.** Proceed

I recommend choosing two areas of your life where you commit to practice on-the-go mindfulness every day for the next week. I am an old-school sticky note enthusiast when it comes to my committed on-the-go practices. Write yourself some reminders and put them around the house, in the car, or at your desk. For a new-school approach, set reminders on your phone.

- **Brushing your teeth:** Since this is something you do every day, twice a day, it makes a perfect mindfulness practice. See if you can pay attention to the experience of brushing your teeth with curiosity and kindness. Notice what other kinds of thoughts come up. Notice resistance. Notice loving it. Just notice. One great way to do this is to try to absorb yourself in feeling the bristles of your toothbrush, the taste and the feel of the toothpaste and how it changes, and the smell too. Pause when you are all done, close your eyes, take a few breaths, and notice how you feel. That is the STOP.

- **Washing your hands:** We are all bound to keep washing our hands a lot. Why not turn this time into a super-tool, not only keeping your body healthy, but also your mind? Let the water run on your hands for a moment and really feel it. Notice the texture and smell of the soap. Notice the way your hands feel as you rub them together and rub in between your fingers. Notice the feeling of rinsing your hands and the feeling of water cascading over your hands. STOP and notice how you feel overall.

- **Chopping an onion:** Any veggie will do, of course, although onions are awesome for this. Feel the papery skin. Notice the colors and textures. Cut into your onion and notice the sensations, colors, smells, and textures of peeling away the outer layer. Notice how you hold your fingers as you hold the onion you are chopping. Notice the action of your hand as it moves up and down with your knife. Notice the sounds of chopping the onion and the sounds around you. Notice tears if they come. At the end, STOP. How was that experience?

- **Putting on your seatbelt:** If you are a person who gets in the car regularly, this is a great one to practice. Put on your seatbelt mindfully. Feel the belt, the plastic buckle, and your bum in your seat. STOP and notice before you pull away.

- **Where else?** The shower? Your daily routine of walking out your door? Taking out the garbage? Tending to your plants? Feeding your cat? Where can you put in one to two minutes of mindfulness that can happen every day in the flow of your day?

It is worth repeating as you get started that you aren't supposed to be good at this. The very act of trying, failing, and trying again is wiring your brain for a more mindful life. Remember these helpful tips as you jump in:

- Be kind
- Let thoughts be thoughts
- You are training a puppy
- Failure is growth

Sometimes I'm ten seconds into my teeth brushing and already I'm rehearsing my 10 a.m. phone call. And so I start again. What does my toothbrush feel like just now? What does the toothpaste foaming feel like right now? And I begin again with the kindness to train this puppy, knowing that every time I leave and return I'm growing my mindfulness muscle.

# Daily Meditation

## So-Hum Meditation

Meditation can be defined in many ways. Here we'll simply define meditation as your formal mindfulness practice—the time you set aside each day to pause, tune in, and ask the mind to focus on a particular thing with kind effort.

This week, you will develop your capacity for mindful awareness with a meditation that includes repeating a sound in your mind as you sit quietly. For some, this process can be more calming for the body and mind than other anchors of attention, which is useful for many who are beginning this journey.

If you have a mindfulness practice and prefer a breath, body, or sound anchor, you are welcome to work with your regular practice.

What is an anchor in meditation? It is just what it sounds like. You know your mind is bound to wander so you give it an anchor, or something to work with. Remember, meditation is not stopping your mind. In the beginning especially, giving your puppy mind a bone to gnaw is helpful—and your anchor does just this.

This week, your anchor is an internal repetitive sound. This is simple: inhale "so" and exhale "hum." Repetition soothes the nervous system. Losing track of the sound and coming back again and again builds new synaptic connections in the brain.

Here's how to get started:

- Settle into your spot for meditation. You might be on a chair, a couch, or even on the floor. I recommend being in an upright seated position instead of lying down. (Lying down is often a signal to the body to sleep.)
- Close your eyes or gently rest your attention at one spot. Take a deep breath in and then exhale. Let your body settle here.
- As you breathe your natural and normal breath, begin to re-peat "so" to yourself as you breathe in and "hum" to yourself as you breathe out. Continue in this way. "So" on your inhale and "hum" on your exhale.
- If you are using the video, that's it. Let my voice guide you. If not, set a timer for five minutes so that you can rest into the practice and not worry about the time.
- Most of us will drift off, maybe every three seconds. Every time you notice you have drifted into thinking, you can smile at your mind and gently bring it back to your so-hum. Remember, it is just like an exuberant puppy that needs a little training.
- When your time is up, pause for a moment. Notice how you feel. What is present? It need not be good, calm, or nice. Just notice what is occurring and allow it to be.

That's it. You just meditated!

How was it? Delightful? Miserable? Do you see how fast the mind is to judge it? Now can you take out the labels and notice what actually happened in the meditation?

- Did you sit still? Did you fidget? (Neither is right or good.)
- Did your mind wander? Did you return? Did it wander again? (Great!)
- Was it uncomfortable? Comfortable? (Either way, you win again.)

We'll talk more later about why it's the practice that matters, and not how successful it feels. Even if you can't focus on that sound for more than two breaths at a time, doing this practice can be a life-changer. In the context of this program, this is the daily brain training that means you'll reach for one of the other tools in this book when push comes to shove, and you will feel like you had a choice rather than just having to react to life from your past conditioning.

# DAILY DE-STRESS PRACTICE

## BRUSH OFF STRESS & CHAIR YOGA

"Fear is the mind killer," goes the line from the book *Dune*. Trite perhaps, but true. Stress is none other than a form of "fight, flight, or freeze" taking over your brain. When we are in that state briefly, or what is called "acute stress," it's fast and furious, giving you a shot of adrenaline, moving blood from your vital organs toward your muscles so you can fight or run, and shutting down the functions of your body that are not essential to fighting off or fleeing from a threat.

If you live in this state long enough it becomes chronic stress. Under sustained chronic stress your body responds negatively. The impact of sustained increases in blood pressure, heart rate, and adrenaline can add up to illnesses such as heart disease, irritable bowel syndrome, insomnia, migraines, anxiety, and depression. In fact, the American Institute of Stress cites various studies stating that 75–90 percent of all doctor visits in the US originate from stress-induced illnesses.

Now consider that most of us live somewhere between acute stress and chronic stress each and every day, without the added concern of a global pandemic and its aftermath. If you were born after 1970 in a country that hasn't been directly affected by war or an act of god on your soil, you are likely living in a time of unprecedented stress for your generation.

And there is good news! Stress can be moved out of your body quite quickly. It may need to happen many times per day, and it is possible.

Stress lives at the level of your nervous system. In fact, all the information you process each day—every sensation, sight, sound, taste, and interaction—must be processed through your brain stem first. This is the oldest part of your brain, or where your "reptilian" brain deciphers if you are safe or not.

This week I offer some quick tools to move the stress through your body. I encourage you to try at least one of them each day. You can even follow along with the videos mentioned in the book.

## Three-Minute Brush Off: Exercise 1

This exercise takes about three minutes total. You can do it sitting or standing. It might seem silly at first, and I'm always shocked at how great I feel when I do this.

1. **Pat your body.** Start at your feet, working up your body, patting all the way up. Take about forty-five seconds to do this. Pat one leg, then the other, working around the front, back, and sides. At your torso, pat all the areas you can reach, including your tummy, lower back, side ribs, upper back, and chest. Then move to your arms, and even do your throat, neck, and head. Pause for a few breaths and notice what you feel.

2. **Squeeze your body.** Again, starting at your feet, gently touch your body with light squeezes (sense what feels best to you), working up to the crown of your head just as you did with the pats. Pause and take a few breaths. Notice all the sensations alive in your body.

3. **Brush your body.** This time, gently brush your body starting at your feet and working your way to the top of your head. Pause and notice the sensations.

4. **Stop.** Close your eyes and linger here for a breath or two. Notice how you feel with kindness and curiosity. When you are ready, open your eyes and be on with your day.

Did you notice your body tingle or pulse? What else did you observe? Not only do I experience a whoosh of sensations and a sense of vitality, but I also feel calmer. This kind of simple rhythmic touch helps move stress out of your body.

Also notice your mind. How do you feel after this? Don't fret if your mind is still racing. These exercises are about moving the buildup of stress out of your body, which will certainly have an impact on the mind as well.

## CHAIR YOGA FOR BACK AND NECK: EXERCISE 2

This quick bit of movement reduces tension in your back and neck. You'll move rhythmically with your breath, which is like a lullaby for an unhappy nervous system. This calms the stress response quickly. Add the mindfulness—observing your experience with kindness and curiosity—and now it's like you're training for an endurance run. You've gone from a screaming baby to an endurance athlete in just a few breaths.

*Part 1: Sit Up Tall*

1. Sit toward the front of your chair so that your feet can rest comfortably on the floor. If your chair is too high for this, place a folded blanket or a hard pillow under your feet.

2. Notice your lower back. If it is rounded toward the back of your chair, sit up as tall as you can. Try to create a natural forward curve in your lower back. This is your lumbar curve, and it is the part of your spine that should be curving forward a little in most people.

3. Draw your ears back over your shoulders. This will feel pretty funny if you've been looking at a screen, or even reading this book. Most of us jut our chins forward. Your neck will be so relieved to stack back up over the rest of your spine.

4. This is your resting place.

*Part 2: Cat and Cow*

1. Place your hands on your knees. Take an inhale to begin.

2. On your exhale, round your spine like a cat. Puff your back toward the back of your chair and let your head hang down and forward. Stretch the space between your shoulder blades as you push them back. You can make your arms straight.

3. On your inhale, pull your elbows back and lift your chest to the ceiling, rounding your spine the other direction. This one is called cow. You can moo if you want. (I'm only half kidding. It's good for adults to do things that feel silly and might make us smile or laugh).

4. Repeat in both directions three to ten times. Stay within a range of movement that feels good to you. There is no need to overdo this movement.

5. Return to resting with your tall spine and stop. Take your breath and notice the impact of this movement and breathing.

*Part 3: Gentle Twists*

You can do this with your arms reaching up or not. I've given the instructions with your arms moving as it is slightly more complex. If you have a shoulder injury or another reason for limited arm mobility, do it in whatever way works for you. That is making a healthy choice. That alone is lovely and enough.

1. As you inhale, lift your spine to the ceiling as tall as you can. Reach your arms up straight above your head.
2. Exhale and twist to your right, staying forward on your bum. Place your right hand on your chair, if possible, and your left hand on your right knee. Look gently toward your right shoulder. *Do not overtwist.* Move within a range of motion that feels good. We are so wired to think more is better. It isn't.
3. Inhale and come back to your center with your arms up.
4. Exhale and twist to the left in the same manner.
5. Repeat three to five times in each direction.
6. Return to resting and stop. Perhaps close your eyes and notice your experience right now as you take a full breath in and out.

*Part 4: Free Your Neck and Shoulders*

1. Start from your resting position.
2. Inhale and reach your arms up. Exhale and bring them down so that you are holding the back of your chair, or interlace your hands behind you near your lower back.
3. Gently pull your chin back over your shoulders.
4. Slightly lift your chin up to the sky and press your shoulders down your back a little.

5. You can breathe there for five breaths, or release after a breath and start from the beginning. Either way, your rhythmic breathing will calm you.

6. Release when ready.

7. At the end, stop. Notice what is present right now for a breath with kindness and curiosity. Then move on.

# KNOW WHAT YOU WANT:
## LESSON 1

So often when we think about our lives, we are quick to say what we don't want. Sometimes this is very clear, and other times we just have a vague feeling of what we don't like, and therefore we spend our lives trying to avoid it.

Imagine trying to drive to a destination this way. You get in the car. You don't have a map for where you want to go because, well, you don't know where you want to go. So you start driving and you evaluate as you drive. "No, not that." "Not that." "Not that." No place is going to be right because you aren't looking for what you want; you're just looking to avoid what you don't want. This is pretty helter-skelter and is often exhausting. It feels out of control, thus spazzing out your nervous system.

Now imagine you have a very clear picture of where you want to end up. You know it's in the mountains, or by the ocean, or it has a farmhouse, or a sweet condo in a city. Right there you've eliminated a whole lot of fuss and wasted energy. You are clearly not driving to inland Texas if you want the ocean.

Our lives are like this. Many of us do not take the time to be clear on what we want. We just keep living, hoping someday we'll be fulfilled. We exhaust ourselves this way and waste the vital energy we could have used to build the lives we want and contribute meaningfully in the world.

One of the quickest ways to feel more fulfilled and in control of your life is to write down what you actually want. This can be scary, I know. Some of you are afraid that saying what you want now will limit you in the future. Some of you will feel like this is selfish, or it's pretty culturally foreign to imagine your life in this way. I understand and respect that.

And writing down what you want is a trick for the mind. You aren't actually in control. It is very likely that you won't get exactly what you want in the way you imagine it. The point is to stop waiting and start giving yourself the direction you need to begin. This calms your nervous system so that you can engage with the changing circumstances of the world graciously and with ease.

Pausing to ask what you really want is also not as selfish as it sounds. First, when human beings (you and me) are fulfilled and deeply happy, we tend to be better citizens. Connecting to what matters most to you can also mean you include things that matter on a bigger scale than just your most personal lifestyle wants. When I stop and imagine what I really want, I see a world where we have done the work to end racism, where all children are cared for, and where we are collaboratively doing the work to right human-caused climate change. And yes, I'd also like to provide for my kid's college and live in a nice house. All these things can coexist.

Defining what you want can be fun and simple. While I've done countless versions of this kind of thing, this one comes from my mentor, Suzanne Conrad of Lightyear Leadership. Suzanne has distilled this important exercise into something quick you can do daily. It's called "The Power of Knowing What You Want."

For this exercise, you'll need five to ten minutes, a piece of paper, and something to write with. It's optional to use colors if they make you happy, and you can put on some music if that feels right too.

Here's how:

- Draw a large circle on a piece of paper.
- Set a timer for five minutes. Inside the circle, write everything you want in your circle. Notice when you censor yourself, and then write those ideas down. When you start to run out of ideas, stay with it. Go the whole five minutes. Sometimes the best things come at the end and will surprise you.
- Next turn your attention to what you don't want in your life. Write that outside your circle. Usually this doesn't require the same discipline as writing what you want.
- Now sit back and read the things inside your circle. As you do, focus on feeling your body. What body sensations do you notice as you read? These are your clues for what you really want. Is there anything in your circle that doesn't belong, or that came from what you thought you should write or want? Is something missing? Is this what you would really choose? Don't leave anything in that circle that you—right now—don't choose for yourself. Edit as needed.

Hang this circle up in front of your desk or in another spot where you'll see it each day. Every day this week spend one minute reading your circle. What's inside? Focus on feeling these things in your body. How does it feel to choose the things in your circle?

For now, you want to cultivate the ability to *feel* what you want in your life—what you choose—and be with it.

You may notice that sometimes you feel a bit sad or fearful that you can't have what is inside your circle. That is so normal. Attend to this with some curiosity and kindness. One way to do that is to practice STOP: pausing, taking a breath, and feeling for a moment. There will be more on working with this sort of thing in the "Cultivating Well-Being" section this week.

After a few breaths, you will shift your focus to imagine yourself living the things inside your circle and allowing yourself to feel them. You don't have to believe it yet or know how yet. Right now you are simply getting used to what it *feels* like to choose what matters to you.

# Break Free from Reaction and Step into Choice: Lesson 2

When you are reacting to anything—how your family is behaving, how other people handle masks or not, how your company rolls out a policy change, this list could go on and on—you are not in a place of power over your own choices.

Reaction robs you of your power and agency. It wastes an enormous amount of your energy, and it doesn't often get you what you need or want. It's normal and it's not very helpful. Never was there a better time for all of us to stop reacting to the world and to others, and to start making empowered choices.

## Get Free of Reaction

What is a reaction? You know you are reacting if you are angry, snapping at others, or withdrawing. What other ways do you react? If you notice yourself spinning out in judgment of those around you, that is also a type of reactivity.

When I react in these ways, I've lost the power to choose what I want. I'm really just stuck in an unhappy, unhealthy cycle.

Luckily you have a reliable built-in barometer to guide you from reaction toward choice: your body sensations. We will call these sensations your "body triggers," and they tell you when you are in reaction or choice.

Try this experiment with me. It will take you about one minute. Some of it will bring up something enjoyable, and some of it will likely be uncomfortable. None of it will last.

## YOUR BODY TRIGGERS: EXERCISE 1

Notice where you are sitting right now. Close your eyes if you like. Notice your body as it is. Notice your breathing as it is.

I simply invite you to notice what sensations, thoughts, and emotions arise for each item below:

- **Biting into a lemon.** Let yourself see and feel yourself biting into a big lemon slice. What happens in your body? Be with it for fifteen seconds or so, then take a clearing breath.
- **COVID-19.** Say that word to yourself and observe. What happens in your body? Your mind? Your emotions? Be with this for a moment. Now take a big breath and return to feeling yourself right where you are. If you need to, place your hand on your heart, open your eyes if you need to, and orient to where you are and what is around you that makes you feel safe.
- Imagine you (or, if it's helpful, a child), running across a field, arms outstretched, laughing. Be with this for a moment. What arises in your body?

These very body sensations tell you when you need to pay attention to things. When you pause and notice pleasant body triggers, you allow them to grow within you. People often report feeling happier when they learn to notice these pleasant sensations. This is a form of mindfulness that lifts your spirits and has a positive impact on your physical well-being too.

Likewise, learning to notice the sensations that are disquieting gives you clues about how to move forward so you're not stuck in them. We experience a range of these unnerving fight-or-flight responses in our bodies each day, yet very rarely do we move them through us unless we get in some exercise. Learning to recognize them quickly in your body gives you a choice to clear them out immediately so they don't compound.

What does this have to do with reactivity? When I've got fight-or-flight built up in my body from an email I've just received—say, in my case, from my yoga studio landlord, and then my kiddos yell at each other—my nervous system is already on edge. I'm far more likely to react than respond in those moments with my kids if I haven't cleared out the first stressor.

Where does this compounded stress happen in your life these days? Have you learned anything in the book so far that might help you move it out of you quickly? And don't worry, more tools are coming.

## DISCERNING BODY TRIGGERS: EXERCISE 2

Let's try another experiment to refine your ability to notice and discern your body triggers. For each bullet point, see if you can feel the body trigger associated with it:

- The sounds of birds singing
- A voicemail from your boss saying, "We need to talk"
- Your mom calling for the fifth time consecutively
- You receive a text message saying, "I appreciate you"
- A baby crying

- Noticing someone had messed up on a work project you expected to have been completed and done correctly
- A quarrel in a small busy coffee shop about current health guidelines from the CDC
- Someone you love saying, "I love you"

Did you notice similar reactive sensations in some of the items above? What were those sensations? These sensations will ultimately help you break free from reaction into choice. Keep going to the next exercise to hone this superpower.

## BODY TRIGGERS BREAK THE CYCLE OF REACTION

Having a reaction means something caused you to act—you did not act of your own free will. Responding, on the other hand, means you chose how to respond to life. One is fight-flight, or freeze-based (stress), and the other comes from clear thinking and knowing.

I want to be clear about this. The goal here is not for you to be an unemotional blob of calm whenever anything happens. There is unkindness and injustice—big and small—in the world that must be addressed. When I react, though, it is from self-preservation driven by my primal brain. Often no one really gets their needs met and positive change is unlikely.

When I move out of reaction, I step into choice. What do I really want here? How am I most likely to get that? What is the best possible outcome for all? I may need to feel and move through the stress response to get to my choice. Once I am in my choice, the executive functioning part of my brain is online and I start to act like an adult living in this adult body. (This is a journey. I think about this stuff all day, and I still react to my husband, and I catch myself sounding like a defensive pre-teen.)

The really cool thing here is that once you are in touch with the body triggers of reaction and the emotions that connect with them (fear, anxiety, worry, guilt, anger, hurt, grief, sadness), you can start to work with them.

For instance, anxiety has been an emotion and a mental state I have noticed often over the last year and a half. When I'm anxious about something and I try to stuff that sensation down and keep plowing ahead, it comes back to visit me in the night. On the flip side, when I think, *Oh, that tightness in my chest and sinking feeling in my belly is anxiety,* I can then work with it. I literally ask myself what it's trying to tell me and what needs to be tended to. Sometimes the answer is that I need to go on a walk or stretch for five minutes. Sometimes the answer is that I need to ask for help or stop trying to control something I can't control.

Here are some clear steps for turning reaction into powerful choice:

- Notice the physical sensation and see if you can name it, i.e. itching on my head, tingling in my hands, constriction in my throat … there are as many possibilities as there are human beings on this planet.
- Ask yourself the questions below. You may need some time with these questions—sometimes moments, and sometimes days. The more you practice, though, you will get good at doing this positive work in a split second.
  - o What is this sensation trying to show me?
  - o What needs tending to?
  - o What must I believe to feel this way?

- Next ask yourself, *What is a nourishing choice right now?* (A nourishing choice is one that aligns with what you want in your life and acknowledges your humanity and the humanity of those around you.)

This third step deserves a little exploration. First, sense into what would nourish you. Is it asking for help? Is it time alone? Would music calm you? Is it clearing out anger and judgment so you can calmly ask the stranger standing close by for some extra space with kindness and compassion?

Sometimes what I need or want is a yoga class or a good, hard run, and that is not an option in the moment. That is where your de-stress tools come in handy. Clear stress and you clear judgment. Then you have freedom to make a nourishing choice.

# CULTIVATE WELL-BEING WITH COMPASSION

Place your hands on your heart, right here, right now. Take a deep breath and feel the weight of your hands. Notice what it feels like to sit like this for a breath or two.

The sensation that you began to conjure in that moment is the feeling of compassion. Compassion is a supercharged tool to help you work with difficulty and suffering.

Compassion is the perfect companion to honing awareness of your body triggers. As you become aware of all the stress and reactivity you may go through in a day, compassion gives you kind ways to nurture yourself and move the reactivity along.

## WHAT IS COMPASSION AND CAN IT REALLY HELP YOU?

Compassion is noticing suffering in a way that opens your heart toward it. You feel warmth, caring, and kindness, and you are less likely to judge yourself or others harshly. Compassion also brings with it the realizations that: a) all beings suffer, and b) our imperfections are part of the human experience. The opposite of empathy fatigue, practicing compassion tends to open a well of energy and a sense of expansion.

Self-compassion is the ability to respond to yourself with the same kindness you would offer to a good friend. Research suggests that when you turn toward yourself—your struggles, your strengths, your emotions, and your shortcomings—with self-compassion, you develop:

- Resilience: the kind of resilience that allows you to stick with difficult things
- A more accurate self-concept
- More caring relationships
- Self-forgiveness
- Less reactive anger

It's easy to get these benefits. Below are a few exercises to help nurture self-compassion, all of which are adapted from Mindful Self-Compassion as developed by Dr. Kristin Neff and Chris Germer. There is a whole course on mindful self-compassion, and I encourage you to explore it more closely if this work speaks to you.

## Like a Good Friend: Exercise 1

For this exercise, you can read it ahead of time and then practice it. It will take about three to four minutes, and is best done where you can close your eyes and feel for a moment.

- Sit comfortably and take a breath or two to settle your body and mind.
- Bring to your mind a friend who is struggling with something, or who has struggled recently. This could be anything from a health issue, to deep dissatisfaction in their job, to losing a pet, or a divorce. See this friend in your mind. Notice how you

feel about this friend and their suffering. Is there anything you would tell this friend about the suffering they are experiencing? What do you want for your friend? How else would you reach out to compassionately support this friend? See yourself doing this now. Take thirty seconds to one minute to be with this friend in your mind's eyes. Notice what you feel both emotionally and physically. Pay close attention to any body triggers or sensations.

- Now turn toward yourself. Where in your life are you struggling? Offer the same kind words to yourself which you had offered to your friend. Offer to yourself the same wants you had for your friend. Pause and experience yourself offering the same compassion to yourself you would offer to your friend. What physical sensations accompany this compassion? Is it difficult for you to be kind with yourself in this way? That can be normal. Spend a minute pausing with this and allow yourself to receive the compassion.

- Now pause. You might like to place your hands on your heart as you take a few deep breaths in and out. Notice your whole body as you breathe.

- When you are ready, open your eyes. If you'd like, take a few minutes to write about what you noticed.

This simple exercise puts you in touch with the experience of compassion you naturally feel for a friend, helping turn toward yourself with that same compassion.

And it's not just nice. Self-compassion is important. As you cultivate compassion for yourself, you expand your ability to work through difficult situations. You become more resilient. You become more powerful in your life.

## A Compassionate Touch: Exercise 2

Compassion includes a real physiological experience, and it stimulates the rest and digest part of your nervous system (the opposite of the fight-or-flight system). You can learn to tap into this, releasing a little of the same oxytocin your body releases when you get a hug from another person.

Take a moment to try different movements and kind self-touch to see what helps you feel connected, cared for, and nurtured. You are looking for soothing body triggers. As you do each one of these, take a breath and practice STOP. Observe and see what's best for you.

- Try placing your hands on your chest, stacked as though over your heart. Take a breath. How does this feel to you?
- Next try giving yourself a hug or squeezing opposite hands to opposite arms in a hugging motion. How does this feel?
- Try squeezing your forearms with your hands. You might start at your wrists and gently squeeze up your arms. What is the experience?
- Try placing your hands on your cheeks. Is this comforting?
- Does something else call to you? You could rub your thighs, cross your arms and place your hands on the back of your neck, or rub your hands together. There is no right or wrong. Experiment to notice what gives you that sense of being cared for.

This little burst of nurturing is something you can give yourself anywhere and anytime, once you are aware of it.

## TAKE A MINDFUL COMPASSION BREAK: EXERCISE 3

This is one of my favorite ways to practice self-compassion, especially when I'm feeling anxiety or fear. It's quite simple, and once you know it, you can do it anytime. Sometimes I do this practice quickly while sitting in the car before I go into a meeting, taking one to two minutes. Sometimes I do this at home and spend a solid ten minutes allowing myself to be with each phase.

- Close your eyes and sit comfortably for a moment. Take a few breaths to settle.

- Notice an emotion, thought, or body sensation that feels difficult. For this exercise I recommend something that feels like a three or four out of ten. (You can always do this with the tens, too, you just may not want to start there.)

- Observe the body sensations connected with this difficulty for a moment, maybe five to ten breaths.

- Next identify the emotion. You might say to yourself, *This is* _____ *(anger, sadness, fear, hurt ... )*. Again, sit with this for a few breaths, acknowledging the emotion and allowing it to be seen.

- Notice where it lives in your body and how it feels. Say to yourself, *This is what* _____ *feels like*. Be with it a moment longer, again observing what is.

- Then say to yourself, *This is a moment of suffering*. Pause for a few breaths, again acknowledging that this is a kind of suffering.

- Lastly, say to yourself, *All beings suffer*. And again, be with that experience. What does it feel like to move through this progression?

This beautiful practice allows you the space to feel what you feel and to recognize our common humanity. This practice alone may be one of the most useful tools you can use as you mindfully emerge anew in the world, developing your well of compassion for yourself and others.

# REFLECT AND CHOOSE

Wow—in just one week, you've traveled a lot of territory. No matter how much of this you've implemented, I'm here to tell you: *good job*. Trust that you've done just the right amount to support you where you are right now.

The intention of this week was to set you up to take back the reins of your life so that you will start to steer your life instead of being thrown about by the circumstances. Part of that is allowing yourself the space to pause and reflect, deciding which of these practices you'll take forward with you.

Here are a few questions you may find useful:

1. What one or two insights did you have this week that felt most substantial?

2. What one or two tools will you carry forward with you, and why?

Taking the time to reflect and choose what is most useful to you leaves you feeling empowered. This is not about me telling you what you need. This is you discerning what is most sustaining for you.

# Week 2:

# RESTORE YOUR INNER STRENGTH

---

This week you will fill your well with a balance of stillness and strength. The set healthy boundaries, and practice making powerful requests.

Strength is often considered to come from force and action. There is certainly action needed in our lives. The question is: where do we source our actions from—fear, love, angst, kindness, reactive anger, or clear sight?

Think back to March 2020. Did you have an experience over the changing restrictions in your community that left you feeling judged by someone for how you were doing it? Was it at the gas pump, or at a restaurant, or maybe you felt like your neighbors were judging you?

Maybe over the course of time you've also been on the judging end of things. You felt people passed too closely in the aisles of the grocery store or didn't wear masks when you thought they should. On the other hand, some of you have felt annoyed that you are required to wear a mask in some places and have judged others for that too.

I think most of us can identify with the experience of judging and feeling judged during the pandemic. And yet we were already doing this before COVID-19, it was just at a quieter frequency. Now it's in our faces. Literally.

Judgment is a human reaction that will continue as we negotiate our way forward in life. As your reptilian brain tries to quickly analyze the safety of every little bit of information it receives, it's doing its best to keep you safe by judging and categorizing. And that's the trick. It is a reaction, and therefore it takes you out of real choice.

What you are doing here is learning to restore yourself to neutral so you can make healthy choices, not reactive ones. Now is the perfect time to nurture this skill, and it will serve you long after your current struggle fades in your rearview mirror. I think of this powerful set of skills as learning to be an adult in an adult body. No more three-year-olds driving this bus.

The practices this week will restore you, cultivating an inner well of stillness and strength that can't be taken away by anyone or any situation. This is intimate strength based in self-awareness and clear direction for what you want. It is strength that comes from pausing before acting, and then acting in alignment with your honest desires and sense of what is healthy for you. It is a self-based power that no one can give you or take from you.

From this self-possessed experience, healthy boundaries become easier to identify, and you put them into action with powerful requests.

# On-the-Go Mindfulness

## Just Like Me

L ast week we played with mindfulness during everyday activities. This week I offer a brief interruption that dampens judgment wherever it may occur. This brings you back to neutral so you can make choices that move you more toward what you really want in your life.

**Just Like Me:** A life-changing mindful compassion practice you can use daily is called "Just Like Me." You can find a link to the long form on the internet at mindful.org/just-like-me-compassion-practice/. As on-the-go mindfulness, I've simplified it, yet it is no less profound. Here's how:

- Whenever you find your body triggers ringing with irritation, judgment, or angst related to, or caused by, another person, repeat these two simple phrases to yourself:
  - o   This person has experienced fear and pain, just like me.
  - o   This person wishes to be cared for and loved, just like me.
- Pause and notice your body sensations now, taking a few deep breaths as you do. That's it!

You are likely to feel a physical shift in your body as you repeat these phrases more and more. Science shows that active compassion practices such as this have a positive physiological impact. The reactions associated with fight, flight, or freeze begin to subside, and the healthy balance of rest and digest restores.

Of course, the more you do something, the more it becomes a habit so that you can pull out this tool when you are in the heat of the moment with someone. It is a real strength that will make a real difference in your life.

I highly suggest putting these phrases on sticky notes or in your phone so you have them handy.

For a big bonus, incorporate this into your day three times each day on a regular interval. Try including some moments when you feel happy, content, or grateful in relationship to another person. You can practice silently with the barista at your coffee shop or the checker at the grocery. You can also expand this practice, editing the phrases in ways that speak to you and help you experience your common humanity.

# DAILY MEDITATION

## BREATH AND BODY SCAN

Daily meditation is the place you come to to get still. In that stillness you develop two key factors for strength. First, the stillness connects you to your inner world and your experience of life. Second, discomfort often arises in the stillness, and you discover just how strong you already are.

Let's look at that first part: stillness as a connection to yourself. By practicing forms of stillness intentionally each day, you give yourself a pause to feel your body, your emotions, and your mind. In this process you discover the very triggers that will take you out while you move through daily life, and you will gain tools to build your strength and stamina to stay powerful in the face of stress.

In this stillness you also cultivate your moment-by-moment awareness. This awareness shows you what you truly feel and need in your life. It can heighten experiences of joy and delight when they occur. On the flip side, when difficulty arises in that stillness, you can make other important discoveries.

When discomfort and struggle arise in your meditation, two magical things happen. First, there is a high likelihood that you'll discover you are already quite strong. You may find you can be with very difficult emotions, thoughts, or body sensations and be okay—maybe not great, but often okay.

Second, you expand your capacity to hold the hard stuff with more ease. Little by little you stay longer with painful emotions or body sensations, noticing them, being kind and curious with them, and always choosing when you are ready to be done.

This is another important component of a regular mindfulness practice—you practice making non-reactive choices each time you become still. When something feels too difficult, you have the choice. Do I want to stay with this longer? Do I feel like I can sit here another minute, and is it healthy? And if you choose, to stop, that is a powerful, valid choice. That act alone develops your ability to make empowered, responsive choices in your daily life. Across cultures and time, focusing on breath and body awareness are contemplative practices that have been taught to help ground people into the present moment. The practices increase focus, a form of strength. This kind of focus is useful everywhere, from helping you complete simple tasks to leading your life from the things you actively choose.

Below, I offer a five-minute breath and body awareness meditation. Beyond the heightened capacity for focus, you may also find this meditation helps you tune into your body's sensations. You may find sensing your body's subtle sensations quite difficult. This meditation gently expands your ability to feel your body. And of course, there are times you feel nothing, and you need not be stressed by that.

If you found the so-hum practice anchored you, you are welcome to stick with it. If you are finding it difficult, this meditation may be more useful to you.

What do I mean by "useful?" Any meditation practice is useful. Sometimes your practice will feel highly agitated; it will feel difficult to focus on your breath or body, and you will be full of thoughts and uncomfortable body sensations. When this happens, this is still a useful meditation practice for two main reasons.

First, the agitation itself is working its way out of your system. Watching it arise and noticing it *without judgment* is the perfect thing to do. It means the stress is less likely to be stuck inside of you, even though sitting through it and noticing it can be quite uncomfortable.

A tip for working with this discomfort is to know it is only going to last for a set time—say, five minutes. You do not have to sit with it indefinitely. And as you learn to sit with the discomfort and be kind to yourself while it's happening, you are wiring new pathways for nonreaction in your brain. Knowing it won't last forever, gently watch the discomfort and see if you can be kind with yourself in the process.

The second benefit to staying when practice feels agitated is that each time you return the mind to your chosen focus of breath (or so-hum), you wire your brain for focus and choice. That is a win, even if it only occurs one time during your meditation.

Having spoken to the benefits of staying through difficulty, I also want to highlight that you are always in control. You always get to choose when the meditation is too much, release it, even shake it out, and move on. You have not failed when you do this. In fact, you have a big win when you:

- Notice your experience in the meditation
- Pause and ask, *Is this healthy right now? Can I sit with this experience with kindness and curiosity and feel safe?*

- If the answer to either of those questions is "no," then you stop. That is a healthy nonreactive choice. Well done!

## MEDITATION

To begin, set yourself up comfortably. Generally, sitting up tall and supporting your back is a great option. If you have a lot of physical pain, you may want to lie down. If it is healthy for you to sit up, that can be helpful, as lying down causes a lot of folks to fall asleep.

- When you are ready, close your eyes and take a big breath in and out. Let yourself settle.
- Begin by noticing your breath. Notice it as it comes in and flows out. Notice how it feels to breathe in and out. Where do you feel your breath most readily? Take about one-and-a-half minutes to watch your breath in this relaxed way.
- After a minute or so, bring your awareness to the top of your head. Notice if you feel any sensations there. You may, and you may not. There is nothing you're supposed to feel. Just notice.
- Move your awareness around your face and notice what sensations are there.
- Next go to your right shoulder and slowly move your awareness down your right arm, eventually to your fingertips.
- Move to your left shoulder and do the same down your left arm. Take your time and move at a pace that feels good to you.
- Return your awareness to your chest and upper back. Notice what you feel in these areas. You might note what you feel—your clothes on your skin, itching, tingling, nothing …
- Move to your lower back and then around toward your belly, again observing and sensing.

- Next move to your right thigh and down your right leg, slowly noticing the sensations present at different areas.
- Move to your left thigh and work down toward your ankle.
- Now notice your right foot: the top, the sides, the bottom. Just observe with curiosity and kindness.
- Observe your left foot.
- Lastly notice your whole body. How does it feel sitting here? What sensations are alive?
- Take one last long breath in and exhale out your mouth slowly.

# Daily De-Stress Practice

## Shake Out Stress

A s we've been talking about, moving stress out of your body is one of the most important things you can do for your well-being. These quick activities renew your energy and stamina. In a brief moment of movement and stillness, you refill your inner well, becoming able to respond to life, rather than react to it. Responding to life from choice is the ultimate strength.

If you take one thing from this course that will make a long-term difference in your life, it is that mini movement breaks are highly effective for moving stress and resetting you back to choice. Yes, I keep saying it because I really want you to remember it long after you put this book down.

Of course, if you have a workout routine, it can do wonders for resetting your nervous system to balance. If you do not have a regular workout routine, or if perhaps you have significant injuries that make that kind of movement difficult, know that even short and gentle movements can make a big difference. While the substantial benefits of regular, longer workouts cannot be replaced, these de-stress tidbits spark some of those same rewards.

The key is that *doing any movement within what is healthy for you is better than doing nothing*. I'll say it again: any movement you do within what is healthy for you is better than doing nothing.

This week I offer very quick things you can do at home while you wait for the water to boil, when you're in the car before you get out, or while at your desk at work. These will be most effective when you choose one or two of these to use consistently, and also decide when and where you will do them for one minimum, three times per day.

## The Practices

- **Tense and release:** Pause wherever you are. Tense your whole body—your hands, arms, face, belly, and legs—and hold your breath for a count of five if you can. Then let go. Spread your fingers wide, open your mouth, and exhale. Then take three normal breaths and notice what you feel.

- **Shake and stomp:** Okay, this one is silly. And it feels so good. You can do it sitting or standing. Stomp your feet hard on the ground and shake your hands and arms for thirty seconds. Relax your head and neck. You'll want to stop before thirty seconds. Keep going. At thirty seconds, stop and take a deep breath. Pause to notice all the sensations in your body. Maybe tingling? Maybe your heart pounding? Maybe your feet throbbing? Notice how alive you feel.

- **Lion's breath:** Again, this can feel a bit silly, and it's worth it. You'll release tension in your jaw and face. To begin, breathe in and scrunch up your face nice and tight. On your exhale, open your mouth wide, stick out your tongue, and roll your eyes up. Do this three times. Then pause and simply notice what you feel for a breath or two.

I encourage you to get family and coworkers on the bandwagon to do these with you. Colleagues appreciate it when we give them a chance to release stress and have a little fun. If you have a roommate, partner, or children, get them to do these with you, and you will all benefit.

# Make Powerful Requests:
# Lesson 3

Asking for what you want with clarity is powerful—for everyone. You move closer to what you need and want, and you stop wasting time in situations that aren't working. Others are empowered in part because they know exactly where you stand and what you'd like. They can either say yes, no, or something in between. You empower both yourself and others when you make clear requests.

An important part of making powerful requests is knowing what you want, and not feeling bad about it. Really hear that: know what you want. Stop being squeamish, or guilty, or uncomfortable about it. Just make your request with kindness and clarity.

The anatomy of a powerful request is simple:

1. Listen for what you need and want
2. Clear out your constricted energy
3. State your request clearly and specifically in the affirmative
4. Pause and check your reaction

You will not always get what you want. Know that. You cannot control the outcome of the requests you make. The magic in making powerful requests is that you have clarity, and once you have information back from another person in the form of their answer, then you have the information you need to make your next choices.

Making a powerful request is not always a linear path either. Sometimes you have to clear out constricted energy again and again. This is important as requests made from anger, judgment, and attachments are less likely to receive affirmative responses.

Let's put this to work for you. What is an area of your life where you need to make a clear request in the affirmative? You may want to start with something small to gain confidence and skill. Of course, you can always jump into the deep end too. Once you settle on an area where you sense a request would benefit you (and maybe others too), start walking through the four steps:

1. **Listen for what you need and want.** Take an area of your life where you sense something needs a change. Pause and notice sensations related to this. Ask yourself what you need or want in this area of your life and then be open to what comes. When something feels off, this is where you want to pause and listen in. Often the presenting issue is not really why you are agitated about it. What is underneath? What do you really want and need? You can use your body triggers to sense when you've hit on what you need to request, as your body will likely feel some release, lightness, and spaciousness.

*A Personal Example: I was cleaning the bathroom. I could feel my blood starting to boil. Why, in the six months we'd lived here, was I the only person who had cleaned a bathroom? Why had my husband quit taking part in this part of our lives? I could sense a whole lot of anger and resentment rising. Body triggers were starting to scream. My chest got tight. My throat constricted. My mind was racing with all sorts of things I was saying to him, but he wasn't even home. A powerful request was in order. I needed to ask for help cleaning the bathrooms. That was clear. Yet, in the agitated self-righteous state I was in, there was no way that was going to be successful.*

2. **Clear out constricted energy.** Constricted energy around what you want and need will block your ability to state your request powerfully. Your constricted energy may mean you could benefit from forgiving yourself or someone else. It may mean you need to let go of judging yourself or another, or both. Sometimes step one of deeply listening for the heart of the matter will clear this energy itself.

Pause. Feel your body. Ask, *Do I have constricted energy to clear about this?* If you do, you can try breathing into it. You can use any of the techniques we've learned so far: mindful observation, de-stress techniques, and compassion. Trust that you know how to clear out the energy. Observe it with curiosity and kindness, and see ask how you can release it.

*A Personal Example: Clearly, when it came to the bathroom, my energy was tied in knots. Not only was my jaw set, but my mind was as well. And it literally felt like my blood was boiling. While this wasn't comfortable, it was great to see. My body triggers and crazy mind were showing me it was time to use my tools.*

*So I stopped cleaning. I paused and I noticed all of those body triggers. I took a few deep breaths and smiled kindly at myself. This is certainly the human condition. I then asked myself, What do I really need? It was in the asking that I found the release of the energy. Steps one and two were directly tied, and you may find this happens for you too.*

*Once I asked what I really needed, I was able to quiet my nervous system and sense what I actually wanted. I wanted—and still want—my husband to be a partner with me in the house, and even more important, I want my daughters to see that dads and male partners clean bathrooms. This feels incredibly important to me. This clear sight calmed the energy, along with a few deep breaths.*

3. **State your request clearly and specifically in the affirmative**. Create a request that is clear, specific, and in the affirmative. Rework it a few times until you can meet all three criteria:

1. **Specific:** The more specific or measurable a request, the easier it is for someone to know if they can agree to it or not.
2. **Clear:** The other person understands what you want. Another word for this is "direct," rather than couching your request in a lot of extra words. When stating your request, keep it to one sentence if possible. If the person asks for more information, feel free to respond with other thoughts while keeping the actual request simple, without extra reasoning or bargaining. Just state your request.
3. **Affirmative:** Ask for what you want, not what you don't want. The brain computes based on what it hears. When you ask for what you *do* want, that is what the other person's brain chews on. If you say what you *don't* want, they have to wade through more thinking. Nature also abhors a vacuum. When you speak about what you don't want, something needs to fill that space. Know what you want, and ask for it so you don't end up with unintended outcomes.
   Inset Story: Once my energy was clear, I was able to craft an honest and kind request. "Would you commit to cleaning the girl's bathroom with them one time per week?" I was able to

deliver this request without being angry or blaming him for what had been happening. My body felt strong and powerful as I spoke. All the constriction was gone. I felt clear, and he sensed that.

Powerful requests can be tricky to craft sometimes. Here are some examples of thoughts turned into requests:

| Thought or Complaint | Request |
| --- | --- |
| *At home ...* | |
| "This needs to change." | **"I request that we add sweeping the kitchen floor as part of dinner clean-up. Can you agree to that with me?"** |
| "I hate it when you leave your hair in the shower." | **"Please take your hair out of the shower when you get out."** |
| And a special COVID-19 favorite: "How are we feeling about the playdate and the current COVID numbers?" | **"Given the current numbers, I request that our kids keep their masks on indoors."** |
| *At work ...* | |
| "They don't give me any opportunities and I need a change." | **"I'd like to contribute _____ to the new project."** |
| "I deserve a raise." | **"I'd like to be making ____ starting on ____ (date)."** |

Notice these are very simple and clear. They leave others empowered to give you clear answers.

4. **Pause and check your reactions before responding**. Sometimes when you make a request, you'll get exactly what you want. Like magic.

Sometimes you'll get a defensive response. Check in with your body triggers before you respond. If you get defensiveness, double back. Clear out the constriction that may flood into your own body. Then, with compassion, restate your clear, specific request in the affirmative. You'll get a lot of mileage out of this.

Sometimes people who will ask for more information or for you to defend your request. Again, check your own reactions. Pause and clear out the body triggers so you can listen for how to respond. Sometimes people have very valid follow-up questions. Pause, notice, and respond. You don't need to overtly anticipate this in your initial request. Let your request be a clear request. Let others respond. Stop managing the conversation.

Lastly, you will also get "no." This is perfect. You have gotten clear information about where someone stands, and that is excellent. Of course, when you hear "no," most of us need to use our practices to clear out the energy of reaction. Once cleared out, you have a choice. What best serves you right now?

> *A Personal Example: I delivered my request to my husband about the bathroom cleaning. He was sort of snarky at first, as he felt a bit defensive. I paused and let him have his reaction. I noticed my own reactions. Then, after a bit, I said, "I'm not blaming you for anything.*

*I would like help with the bathroom cleaning each week, and I think it would be awesome if our girls know you help. If you helped them, which would be a great way to show them they can expect men in their lives to be partners in this way. Given this, are you willing to start cleaning the bathroom with them once a week?" He said yes, and he even put it in his phone reminders.*

Learning to make powerful requests has helped me immensely over this last year with everything from social gatherings to negotiating a lease for my yoga studio.

In fact, just today, even as I was editing this part of the book, I had a scheduled call with my landlord. My yoga studio has been closed for over a year in the city of Seattle with a four thousand square foot space. We are trying to create a new lease. We are close, and I have one major sticking point. I felt tightness in my chest and an overall dread in my body.

Instead of avoiding it, I paused and I asked, *What is this trying to tell me?* In that moment, I realized that all there was to be done was practice making a powerful request. Next I asked, *What do I really need?* From that, I formulated my clear request in the affirmative. My chest loosened, my jaw loosened, and I felt lighter. Holding the stress had been a waste of my time and energy.

Once we got on the phone, I simply stated what I needed to move forward. I was honest and straightforward, and it was simple. No games. No wasted time or energy. It was friendly and clear. He said, "I hear you. Let me see what I can do."

So go forth and try this. It is ultimately kind and honest to make these kinds of requests, and it will leave you feeling more powerful in your life.

## CHART FOR MAKING POWERFUL REQUESTS

| Topic: | | | |
|---|---|---|---|
| Listen: What do you want/need? | Clear out constricted energy | Make a request | Pause and check reactions |

| Topic: | | | |
|---|---|---|---|
| Listen: What do you want/need? | Clear out constricted energy | Make a request | Pause and check reactions |

# SET HEALTHY BOUNDARIES: LESSON 4

W e—the world—have never lived through this moment in time before. No one has the rules. And while everyone may have very strong opinions, no one knows exactly how to do this. Just as every spring the world is different than the previous spring, emerging from any difficult time or transition means there are new rules for your new world.

This may be both exciting and terrifying. However it feels, it is a new world, and that means you have a role in creating it. Anything new brings with it an opportunity for you to define how it can look for you. You are not at the whim of all that is happening around you.

This is where boundaries come in. You have an opportunity to get really good at setting healthy boundaries and developing deep respect for others in the process. Healthy boundaries highlight our humanity and are meant to help us all flourish. Healthy boundaries are set from what you want, not from fear and anxiety.

That is worth repeating: *healthy boundaries are set from what you want, not from fear and anxiety.* If you set boundaries from anxiety, you are reacting. Reaction begets more reaction. This is an agitated state that weakens your well-being and mental clarity. It exhausts you.

A healthy boundary helps you create what you want in your life. It is based in love, compassion, and clarity. It comes from your inner stillness, and you feel stronger.

So how do you set a healthy boundary? Healthy boundaries have a few key elements to them:

- They are proactive. They set you up to get more of what you want out of life, rather than reacting to what you don't want.
- When you imagine your healthy boundaries and live by them, your body triggers are generally expanded and settled (versus being constricted or agitated).

When building your mindful life anew the way you want it, boundaries are both things you consciously invite into your life and things you need to clear out of your life. Healthy boundaries may be physical, emotional, work-related, and more.

Boundaries need to be reset often. In a way, they are a mindfulness practice in and of themselves. You see what you need, recognize where you've been pulled out of what you want, and you reset the boundaries. That is it. There is no anger. No shame. No guilt. No drama.

See clearly. Set the boundaries you need to create the life you desire. *Healthy boundaries are based in choice and are free from reaction.*

While there are many ways to set boundaries, I offer three different practices to set boundaries here. Feel free to skim this section and see what you want to work with this week. Then choose one of these exercises and take it on.

## HEALTHY ENERGETIC BOUNDARIES

You know how some people walk out of a room and it just feels icky? Conversely, there are people who seem to light up a room. We all have an energetic wake, and it's helpful to check in with yourself regularly to see if there is anything that needs to move closer or farther out of your energetic space. Has something left an energetic residue on you that it's time to move along, or does something need to come a little closer into your world?

I know, this might sound a little woo-woo, and I've found that it can make a difference in how much energy I have for the things that matter in my life when I clear out the gunk.

You can do this quick exercise every morning or evening, and on an as-needed basis throughout your day. This process can take as little as one minute. I've adapted it from one of my teachers, Susanne Conrad, and her work through Lightyear Leadership and GeoTran (in that work, it is called a "boundary shield").

Here's how:

- To start, think of yourself as having energetic rings that expand out from your heart, like the rings on a tree.
- Ask yourself, is there anyone or anything in the area of family that needs to move closer or farther out from your heart? Trust yourself and simply move this person or thing in or out, closer to your heart, or farther away. Notice how that feels in your body. Feeling this energetically in your body is the key.
- Check in again. Is there anyone or anything else in the area of family that needs to be moved in or out? Do that as many times as you need. Again, trust what you hear, and feel it in your body.
- Do the same thing for both the areas of:
- Work, or however you spend the majority of your time, such as being an at-home parent, volunteering, and so on;

- The world, such as your expanded community, politics, global issues, the news, and so on.

Folks generally have a lot of questions about this simple exercise. They worry others will know they have moved them farther from their inner circles. They feel guilty, and more.

Don't overthink this. Check in and trust what comes to mind. No one else needs to know you moved them in or out, and you can always move them again the next day. No big deal. This is about your energetic boundary, period.

Here are some examples: Once, when speaking with an employee at my yoga studio, I could sense her angst about a project. I asked her, "Is Be Luminous Yoga too close in?" She paused and thought about it. She said it was fairly close, and I noted that even as the owner I felt like I had the yoga studio farther away from my heart. I invited her to move the company out from her heart. She imagined that and felt relief instantly.

On the flip side, just yesterday I did this exercise and immediately sensed that I needed to bring my husband closer. I'm so busy with a lot of good work right now, and he is the one I push away. Moving him energetically closer made me smile. When he walked in the door that evening, we had fun together and both felt more connected than we had in a while.

Again, don't overthink this. It's simple. Check in and notice what you notice. Trust what you sense and move things in and out as you need to. You'll *feel* the difference.

|  | Move out | Move in |
|---|---|---|
| Family and close community |  |  |
| Work (or where you give a lot of your time) |  |  |
| Political issues, expanded community, and global issues |  |  |

## LEARN TO SAY "NO THANKS" WITH JOY

When you know what you really want and what is important to you, it becomes much easier to say no to things with ease and grace. One great area in which to practice saying "no thanks" is with your schedule.

Many folks I speak with struggle with full schedules that leave them feeling overwhelmed and depleted. When they look through their calendars, they individually like much of what they are scheduled for. Put together, it's often too much.

The same goes for our stuff. Individually, each thing in my house may seem useful and may have a purpose. And when I realize I'm spending yet another part of my weekend organizing the kid's toys and trinkets and clearing out the garage, I start to feel resentful of all the stuff.

Learning to say no to activities and things in a healthy, happy way comes from your clear connection to what you really want in life. From clarity about what matters most to you, it becomes easier and easier to know what to say yes to and what to say "no thanks" to.

To begin, let's start with seeing where you can clear out some things that will free up your time, energy, and space for the things that matter to you, rather than what you've just accumulated. After that, you can apply this same methodology each day to decide what goes on your calendar and what doesn't, what stuff comes into your life, and what doesn't, and so on.

- Look at your schedule for the next week. Is there something you are dreading? Is it feeling too full? Is it overwhelming? Or maybe it feels just right. That's awesome. Again, your body is the perfect barometer for what is right for you right now.

- If you are feeling a bit tight about your schedule, take a deeper look. Is there one thing that stands out and you know from your body's sensations that it needs to be canceled? Or do you need to clear out a few things? Pause and imagine what it would be like to decline these events. Picture yourself, with clarity and ease, letting people know you will not be able to attend or that you need to change your plans. How is it going to feel to say "no thank you?" It should feel lighter, or perhaps more open or lifted. If not, keep checking. Perhaps some things really need to stay, while others can be cleared.

- Now, with that clear energy, act on what you see. Give yourself a by-when within the next forty-eight hours to follow through. When you speak to people with honesty and ease about your choices, you will find they are generally happy to support your well-being.

- Once you have completed each communication, pause again and notice. Notice how good it feels to say "no thank you" without anger, irritation, or guilt.

In the scenario above, we looked at saying no thanks to external obligations like that obligatory work thing, or that PTA commitment you said yes to and knew you should not have. What's cool is that you can set healthy boundaries with yourself, your loved ones, or in any area of your life with this same process.

I've finally learned at forty-five that when I just say what I mean and need with my mom, everyone is happier, including her. I check with my body before I speak, and I get clear on what is authentic for me, and we all feel better. (And trust me, I have a lot of PTSD about disappointing my mom. It's not her fault, and I used to live in total fear of this. It was all reaction-based, and there was no choice in it for her or me.)

This method works brilliantly for setting boundaries for yourself too. Many of my clients only half joke that they need to start saying no to that late-night Amazon shopping or that second helping of ice cream that's calling. A battle of willpower in the mind often fails and leaves people feeling exhausted, sad, and as though they have failed. Instead, when you pause and ask your body what you need right now, it knows. When you follow that, it's easier to make healthier choices that leave you feeling happy in all ways. When I do this for a week consistently—asking my body, *Is this choice best for me right now?*—my whole life feels more within my control, and thus I feel liberated.

*Stop right here!* If you just started saying "no thanks" with ease, your life would feel better. Maybe this is the only boundary tool you need right now. You choose.

## Turn Complaints into Healthy Boundaries

Your body is constantly giving you signals, and not just that you are hungry, thirsty, or turned on. All day long your body is sending you subtle information about what is healthy and right for you. When you listen, you discover that your body's sensations are firmly rooted in knowing what you want and how to make it happen.

It becomes easy, joyful, and expansive to ask for support and set healthy boundaries from this wisdom. It's like you are putting in the guardrails to help you get to the life you know you want and the life you are here to live.

Often, you know when a boundary is needed because there is an underlying complaint and the pent-up stress that accompanies it in your body. Just this morning, I noticed an irritable tightness in my chest, throat, and hands. I then realized I was muttering to myself that every surface in my kitchen and dining area was covered in stuff— toys, computers, papers, art. I clearly needed a boundary around this.

Can you think of a complaint you have in your life right now? How does it feel in your body? This could be at work, at home, with yourself, with your kids, or anything. And this is the perfect place to set a boundary.

In this exercise you get the opportunity to turn some of those complaints into healthy boundaries using your body triggers and your newfound superpower of making requests. With these ingredients, you learn to listen to the messages in those body triggers of angst and constraint. Instead of pushing those uncomfortable sensations down or trying to work around them, you notice them, listen to them, and turn them into tools to create ease and freedom in your life.

Here are some real-life examples from some of my clients. Notice that a request to yourself can take the form of a commitment. It's quite powerful. Requests and commitments both have a "by when" and clear conditions of satisfaction.

| | Body Trigger & Complaint | Request |
|---|---|---|
| Example 1 | Body Trigger: **Tightness in my chest, throat, arms and hands, itchy**<br><br>Complaint: **"Ahhhh! There is so much stuff in the kitchen. There isn't even a clean surface. I'm going nuts."** | With Who: **My husband and my mom, who is helping us with the kids right now**<br><br>Request: **"I feel really stressed when every surface in our kitchen and dining area has stuff on it all day. I request that each of us helps the kids clean up their items before they leave for school each day and before they go to bed. Can you help me help the kids clear the counters each morning and evening?"** |
| Example 2 | Body Trigger: **Heavy shoulders, pit in my stomach, sinking in my chest**<br><br>Complaint: **"I feel overwhelmed about the work on my plate. They keep piling things on."** | With Who: **Team or boss**<br><br>Request: **"I request that we keep track of these projects clearly so that we can see if we've allocated enough time and resources. I will chart these out and I request that we review these projects and due dates at our weekly meeting. Will that work for you?"** |

|  | Body Trigger & Complaint | Request |
|---|---|---|
| Example 3 | Body Trigger: **My hips, shoulders and back hurt, my chest feels gripped**<br><br>Complaint: **"I'm not getting enough exercise. I'm sitting too much of my day and I'm annoyed that I'm not taking time for myself."** | With Who: **Self**<br><br>Commitment: **I commit to plan my schedule each Friday for the next week, scheduling in my workout times and blocking them out on the calendar.** |

Now it's your turn. Begin by making a list of one to three complaints you have and the body triggers associated with them. After you have that part, identify the request or commitment with your clear "by when" and conditions of satisfaction. Then pause and notice how that request feels in your body. Can you imagine delivering that request with ease?

|  | Body Trigger & Complaint | Request |
|---|---|---|
| 1) | Body Trigger:<br><br>Complaint: | With Who:<br><br>Request: |
| 2) | Body Trigger:<br><br>Complaint: | With Who:<br><br>Request: |
| 3) | Body Trigger:<br><br>Complaint: | With Who:<br><br>Request: |

At the core of this exercise, you listen to your body's wisdom to guide you, and you turn that mindful awareness into clear requests and actions. Like everything else in this book, the more you practice this skill, the easier it becomes.

Once you get the idea of how to do this, you can use this tool daily. Sometimes I practice this tool when I'm deciding what to do first in my workday, or if I'm deciding if I really want a coffee or not. I simply ask, *Is this healthy for me right now?* I listen for my body's wisdom and then act or make a request as needed. The more you practice with low-stakes choices and boundaries, the easier it is when the stakes feel higher—say, when you are deciding to change jobs or when your relationship is struggling.

# CULTIVATE WELL-BEING WITH GRATITUDE

Practicing gratitude is widely documented to increase happiness, positive relationships, and general well-being. Research from the Greater Good Science Center at UC Berkeley suggests it also has positive physical benefits, including decreased aches and pains, less congestion, and fewer headaches.

As a mindful reentry tool, gratitude is a quick, simple tool that reframes your thinking from lack and fear toward contentment and peace. You can feel it in your body, and you can feel an emotional shift, often quite quickly.

Like compassion, it is not about glossing over your real struggles. Instead, gratitude can provide relief from the rumination on what is not working and can be a reset for your nervous system. These positive effects can make it easier to tackle what needs your energy and attention. Gratitude provides a real burst of strength when things feel challenging, painful, and heavy.

To magnify your gratitude practice, approach it as though it is a mindfulness practice. Allow yourself the time to pause and notice how you feel before and after. If you do practice with someone else, share the emotional and physical experience.

Below are three simple practices for gratitude:

## THREE THINGS

This can be done anywhere, anytime. Commit to three times per day—maybe aligned with your meals—to pause and identify three things you are grateful for. They need not be big. Notice how you feel before and after. You may not notice a big shift right away, and that will likely change with more practice.

## DINNERTIME GRATITUDE

Tear up some scratch paper and put it next to a jar on the dinner table. During dinner, have everyone put three things into the gratitude jar, sharing as they go. Then, at the end of the week, reread everything in the jar. It feels amazing! Start your next week fresh.

Headed out for dinner or drinks with friends? Forget the paper and invite your friends to play along. Ask them to share three specific things in their week for which they are grateful. Now you get to learn about what's important to them while all of you get the benefits of a gratitude boost.

## WRITE A THANK-YOU LETTER

Any thank-you letter increases your gratitude, and for this exercise I encourage you to think of someone who has made a real and deep difference in your life. Consider writing them a note, being specific about what they did or gave you, and acknowledge the positive impact this had in your life with as many particulars as you can. Writing this note snowballs the impact of their gift and gives you both a powerful shot of joy and connection.

In my life, I can think of many of these letters I could write. I recently sat down and wrote one to my father-in-law, and then to an acquaintance who took me under her wing. In the case of the latter, I was blown away as I traced the good that had come from one simple thing she said to me as I was starting my yoga studio. And she was, too, once she received that letter.

# REFLECT AND CHOOSE

Well done. You've used some—or all—of the tools in Week 2, and hopefully you are feeling stronger and clearer, and feeling like you have some skills for restoring yourself.

Take a few minutes now to reflect, witnessing what you've learned and what has been most helpful to you.

Here are a few questions you may find useful:

1. Were you able to restore yourself even once when you felt stress arise? How? (And know, that is a *big win*. Good job.)

2. What insights did you have from thinking about powerful requests and healthy boundaries? Is there anything you will carry forward with you?

3. How do you see mindfulness growing, even in baby steps, in your life? What is the impact?

# Week 3:

# MOVE FORWARD WITH EASE

W elcome to Week 3, where you will focus on moving forward with ease. If you are like me, I hear the word "ease" and I say, "Yes, please. How do I get me some of that?"

The truth is, when you apply the tools in this book, more of your life will flow with ease. Yes, unexpected circumstances will thwart you sometimes and you'll get derailed from time to time. *The question is: how can you maximize the conditions for more ease and flow in your life no matter the circumstances?*

The tools you've been practicing will help you move quickly from the stress response toward steadiness and calm. Maybe one day you will become a Jedi master at this skill. I know I'm not there yet, and the more I practice, the more effortless it is to neutralize myself when I get off kilter and I can return to a mindful, easeful flow in my life.

There is a key principle found in mindfulness called nonattachment. All the practice you've had learning how to observe without judgment so far is wiring your mind for less attachment. You see clearly, and you make choices that serve your goals and intentions with less drama. This gives way to more ease in your life, lifting stress away and giving you back a sense of choice in your life.

At the same time, you are making more concrete choices about what you want in your life. In that way, you have clearer aim toward what you want, and maybe even a sense of commitment. How, you might ask, can I be committed to what I want without being attached to it? Aren't those one and the same?

Commitment is a form of focus and dedication. This is useful. Focus is handy when it comes to getting a task done or seeing a creative project through. Yet commitment need not be attached.

Attachment is a form of constriction. Attachment narrows your ability to see clearly and absorb shifts in the world around you. Attachment clings, constrains, and limits. Creativity is dampened, along with your ability to see your choices. Attachment also causes physical contraction, triggering forms of stress in the body.

Imagine a river. When the river narrows, it rushes and tumbles. It feels frenetic. Yes, there are times when you need to be quick and busy and move rapidly, and too much of that lifestyle is a death sentence— literally, in some cases.

When a river is wide, it has plenty of space to lazily flow forward yet it is powerful enough to carve the Grand Canyon. This is the power of steady, gentle nonattached commitment.

*Nonattachment is the ability to align each action in your life toward your commitment and surrender the outcome.* As you move through the exercises this week, I encourage you to practice nonattachment at each turn.

Like all of this work, nonattachment takes practice, but it ultimately gives you freedom and flow. It opens a well of untapped energy that wants to flow through you. It is certainly the most difficult of all the tools we've practiced thus far, and I guarantee you, it can give you the greatest peace and power you've ever felt in your life.

Here are some ways to practice nonattachment this week:

- Stop being attached to mindfulness practice being calm or easy. And when you notice that you are doing this, pause, smile to yourself, and say, *I'm grateful to practice just as it is right now.*
- Bring curiosity into your day. Anywhere you feel yourself beginning to constrict, try being curious about it. Ask yourself, *Why do I feel this way? What must I believe to feel this way? What am I clinging to that has me feeling this way?*
- Practice compassion. Place a hand on your heart and acknowledge, *Oh, this is what attachment feels like. All people feel attached sometimes.*

The trick here is naming it to tame it. And the more you practice, the more freedom you will find. You might even begin to laugh at yourself some.

It's human nature to be attached to outcomes, and it's possible to gain freedom from it.

I also want to be clear that I'm not asking you to become a doormat. On the contrary, when I stop being deeply attached to specific outcomes or behaviors, I open up vast amounts of energy I can put to work in service of my commitments.

Let's take racial justice as an example. It's complex. I don't know how to do it right or well. I do know that I am 100 percent committed to being the generation that says no more to the racial injustice our country has stood on for years. But if I am attached to specific outcomes along this path, I may miss opportunities for greater, more empowered change along the way.

I keep my eyes on the big goal here, and I'm open to opportunities that can move the needle on the issues at hand. As a white woman, I've certainly made my missteps and felt it painfully. Then I do the work to clear out the barbs and body triggers so I can get back to work. I align my energy and my actions toward my commitment.

I am aware that even bringing up the words "racial justice" likely has some folks feeling a lot of body triggers. What a cool opportunity to notice what you are feeling and practice mindful curiosity and committed nonattachment right now. What I find when I do this is that I have little to defend. Committed nonattachment means I'm available in difficult areas of life, rather than needing to react.

This idea of having nothing to defend brings us to another layer of committed nonattachment: the attachment to looking good and doing it right. Again, the sphere of racial justice is a good one for making sense of this. If I'm attached to doing it right or proving I'm a good person, I'm going to get taken out. Surrendering my attachment to looking good means I center the other person's experiences, and I can stop making it about me. In this example, the work is about elevating the lives of people of color. I can notice how my body triggers react to various ideas, policies, and conversations, and then listen for how to support what I'm committed to. I have nothing to defend.

With all this said, it's important to remember that emotions and reactions such as anger, fear, and grief have a place in our lives. They guide you to act on what matters to you. The intention of this book is to learn to kindly address these experiences so they are useful rather than destructive.

Developing committed nonattachment in your life means you steer the ship of your life. Rather than being at the whim of your emotions and experiences, you quickly process them and harness their positive potential. You learn to feel all your feels, and then get to work with joy in your sails. This is the promise of committed nonattachment.

As you launch into Week 3, I encourage you to take your committed nonattachment with you. Commit to a daily practice of mindfulness either as on-the-go mindfulness or as your five-minute seated practice. Stick with something from a previous week if it's working for you, or try something new that is offered below.

Do set aside a bit of time to explore the lessons this week on leading from commitment and beginning again. They are pretty quick and will set you up nicely to see where to head next.

This is a great place to practice committing without being attached. Enjoy!

# On-the-Go Mindfulness

## Real Life Non-Attachment And Commitment

Picture this. You get up early one morning (whatever early is for you). You pour your cup of coffee or tea. You smell it. You are looking forward to drinking the warm liquid cupped between your hands and then settling in to do your five minutes of daily meditation. You have the perfect start to your day all cued up.

Then something has you look at your phone. You realize you forgot your early morning dentist appointment. You are not yet late, but you will be if you don't rush out the door now. Not only that, but you have a project due in three hours which you thought you had time to complete. It will not be done on time and your whole team is depending on you so they can move forward. (Can you feel fight-or-flight rising in your body even now?)

Well, this was my real morning. Granted, the deadline was with a small internal team, but not completing my work had a real impact on their workflow. There went my planned morning, and now I just felt stressed, irritated, and guilty.

Life is like this. You have a plan, a good plan, and it gets ripped out from under you. Do I stop being committed to having lovely mornings? Do I cease my commitment to my meditation because it gets interrupted? No. My commitment to the things that nourish my soul—quiet mornings, mindfully sipping my coffee, and doing my meditation practice—all matter to me. When it all falls into place, I feel on top of the world. I'm in my flow.

So what happens when things fall apart? I'm acutely aware that it is my attachment to the outcome of my morning that could have pulled me off kilter for the day if I had let it. I expressed my frustration to my husband. Of course, this did not clear the body triggers. So as I sat in the dentist chair, I closed my eyes and asked myself, and took a few deep breaths.

I asked myself what I was committed to, even while sitting in that chair. The answer, in that moment, was having a joyful day, no matter how it went or the tasks at hand. Yes, I could feel put out by this change of plans. I could berate myself for messing up the appointment date, and instead I decided instead to be compassionate. I was more committed to having joy in my day than letting this take me out.

This might seem like a silly example, yet can you see that these little attachments along the way add up in a day? If you have three or four experiences like that in a day, let alone ten of them, what happens in your nervous system? Being attached to being perfect, never messing up, never having plans change, or the like does not serve us.

And so we practice seeing our attachments and *choosing* if they serve our commitments.

Use this simple practice throughout your day to foster committed nonattachment. I encourage you to practice this tool intentionally for a few days, maybe at breakfast, lunch, and dinner, making it easier to reach for it when things get difficult and you could really benefit from it. As we've talked about before, I recommend sticky note reminders or setting reminders in your phone. This whole thing can take you less than a minute.

1. Ask, *Where have I been attached to an outcome so far today? What did that feel like? What were my body triggers?* Pause and notice for three to five breaths.

2. Now listen for what is important to you that is causing this attachment. You can ask, *What matters to me most? Is this attachment serving what I'm committed to?* Again, pause for a few breaths, even after you sense an answer.

3. If it feels right to let the attachment go, picture yourself doing just that. You might even imagine holding the attachment in your cupped hands and then blowing it away like a dandelion seed puff.

4. Restate to yourself, *I am committed to …*

Practicing this regularly this week means you'll be more likely to use it in the heat of the moment. This tool certainly came in handy this morning for me.

# Daily Meditation

## Loving Kindness

We've been talking about your mind as a puppy these last few weeks, with the intention of fostering kindness toward yourself and your mind, gently teaching it to come, sit, and eventually stay.

As you develop your mindfulness muscle, your mind feels less and less like a puppy, turning instead into a regal self-possessed lion.

Picture a lion sitting in the sun, looking out across the savanna. It observes its domain, appearing quite in control of its surroundings. It is the epitome of strength, power, and choice. Feel yourself as this lion. Imagine you can feel this way in your body right now.

This is exactly what you've been doing: developing your ability to see clearly and observe with kindness and curiosity. Instead of reacting to every trigger that comes your way, you're beginning (or beginning again) to discern what truly matters to you, putting in place mature tools to foster those commitments.

When you've practiced curious, kind observation, you may have noticed you were less constricted physically and mentally. This sense of spaciousness is an experience of ease. It's not always available, yet you cultivate your capacity for ease in action every time you practice mindfulness.

This week, your attention-based daily mindfulness is meant to expand that sense of ease through loving kindness. This is a focus-enhancing practice. As you repeat phrases of well wishes for yourself and others, often the mind settles and the body eases.

Through this meditation practice, you will:

- Provide the mind with an internal verbal anchor
- Develop focused awareness
- Nurture the physical and mental experience of loving kindness and well-being

I offer the traditional phrases and practice of loving kindness below, and I encourage you to create different phrases if they feel more nourishing to you. The traditional word for this loving-kindness meditation is *metta*. It is a Pali word and comes from the Theraveda Buddhist tradition.

## Loving Kindness Meditation

To begin the meditation, sit comfortably. You'll begin by repeating the phrases of loving kindness silently to yourself three times each, pausing and allowing yourself to feel them in your body. You then move outward from yourself, eventually to all beings.

I've outlined the full process through six different people. Feel free to begin small, maybe just with yourself, and then move outward as you are able. Check in with yourself each day. What is right for you right now?

1. Yourself
2. A loved one or friend (or a pet)
3. A benefactor (someone who has helped you in some way)
4. A neutral person

5. A difficult person
6. All beings

The traditional phrases are offered below. Again, you are welcome to change them. Perhaps "May I be loved" is more nourishing to you, or "May I be free from suffering." You choose.

For yourself:
- May I be happy.
- May I be healthy, in body and in mind.
- May I be safe from inner and outer harm.
- May I live with ease and well-being.

For others:
- May you be happy.
- May you be healthy, in body and in mind.
- May you be safe from inner and outer harm.
- May you live with ease and well-being.

For all beings:
- May all beings be happy.
- May all beings be healthy, in body and in mind.
- May all beings be safe from inner and outer harm.
- May all beings live with ease and well-being.

End by pausing and feeling your body for a moment. You may feel heavy. You may feel light. You may feel peaceful and spacious. You may feel tender. You may notice your heartbeat. You may notice tingling in your arms or hands. It is all good. It is you, being just as you are in the moment with loving kindness.

# Daily De-Stress Practice

## Body Giggles

All this talk about committed nonattachment, setting healthy boundaries, and making powerful requests may have you tensing your muscles. Some part of you likely resonates with these things, and yet, even I feel my jaw tighten as I type those words. Healthy boundaries sound big. Powerful requests sound a little scary. And committed nonattachment, well, that just sounds hard, even if it sounds nice.

This is where those de-stress practices come in. Often we think mindfulness is serious, and we get really heavy about it. And yet at the core of all mindfulness practices, we expand our ability to see that while there is suffering and sadness in the world, there is great beauty and lightness too.

I'll never forget being in the presence of Desmond Tutu and the Dalai Lama. They were both in their eighties at the time, weathered men who had lived a lot of life in the midst of big political chaos and had witnessed deep suffering. They easily danced between tears in their eyes, holding great tragedy in one moment, and laughing hysterically in the next as they joked with each other. The whole point of this work is that you have access to joy and lightness of being while being fully human.

That is why I love these daily de-stress practices. They literally lighten your physical load, moving stress through you and shaking it out.

In that spirit, this week I offer you a sweet and invigorating de-stress movement you can do while standing at the kitchen sink, when you are alone in an elevator, or with your team if you can get them unglued from their chairs. It's called a "body giggle," and was taught to me by my dear friend and colleague, Tina Templeman.

Here's how to body giggle:

- Stand up and just bounce for a moment. Let everything get loose.
- Jump up (leaving the ground if that is healthy for you, or just raise your heels if it's not).
- On your way down, breathe out through your mouth and shake your hands, arms, torso, and head.
- Repeat two or three times.
- Stop. Close your eyes and take a breath. Proceed.

# Lead from Commitment:
# Lesson 5

Leading from commitment is life-affirming and inspiring. But what does that really mean, and what am I suggesting you commit to?

Much of the time we live our lives based on what we don't want, rather than what we do want. We half-heartedly yearn for what we think we want, and we spend a whole lot of energy thinking, *No, not that. Not that. Not that ...*

Living from commitment is about keeping your visions, desires, and dreams squarely in front of you. They become your compass from which you steer with firm, loving, committed nonattachment. Take a breath and let that sink in: firm, loving, committed nonattachment. Does your body have a sensation when you imagine that?

Commitment is not something you do once in your life. I discovered at a young age that commitment is choosing something again and again, even when I didn't want to or when it seemed hard. Your commitments can of course evolve and change. But seeing your commitment as a choice to keep choosing something can be a very freeing way to look at commitment.

Leading your whole life from commitment is like this too. You get to keep choosing what matters to you, clearing out the things that would keep you from these commitments for yourself. Things will get in the way of your commitments. Life circumstances (can you say "pandemic?") will create obstacles big and small. The opportunity is to lovingly and firmly keep choosing what you are committed to.

Throughout this program you've refined your vision—what you want and what is important to you. This is where you are aiming. It's your commitment to yourself.

You don't need to force your commitment. You don't need to strive for it or cling to it. *You need to keep choosing it.*

How? See it. Feel it. Know it. The most impactful thing you can *do* to bring your commitments to life is to keep them present and to align your actions and choices with what you want.

This is in fact a simple process. Every time you come to a choice—big or small—pause. Notice your body sensations. Make choices that align in each moment with your vision. Choices might take the form of requests or saying no. Choices might take the form of action. Choices might take the form of nonaction.

Your life right now is the sum total of all your experiences and choices that have led to this moment. Outside factors beyond your control have influenced your life, and things within your control have influenced your life.

From now on, you have the moment-by-moment possibility of choice. The more you practice the tools in this program, they become part of you and will allow you to stay true to your vision with ease.

You are ultimately the leader of your life. No one else is going to lead you toward your vision and dreams. Leading from commitment means you keep your vision front and center, and that is the map for how you respond to life.

Here is a simple process for leading your life from commitment:

- Distill a list of your top three to five desires for your life from your circle in the "Power of Knowing What You Want" section. These are the things you commit to for your life.

- Post them at your desk, in your car (if you have one), over your kitchen sink, or on your mirror.

- Each day, read them through and pause. Notice any sensations of constriction that may creep in. Maybe even name them. Invite those sensations to pass with ease. Do not force them.

- As the constriction quiets, take a moment to see and feel yourself in the experience of each of the items on your list.

- Quietly ask yourself, *How can I step into this today?* Do not expect specific steps of problem-solving ideas. Some may come, and you are asking your inner knowing for guidance. That guidance often comes from quiet intuition, not from your thinking mind. Sometimes the guidance says, "Be still," or "Be patient." Sometimes you'll sense, "Sign that agreement today," or "It's time to ask for that raise."

Throughout the day, as you make choices at each turn, you align your choices more often and more easily with your commitments for yourself. When you are faced with big choices in your life, you may run through the activity above and then ask yourself what is right for you. Listen for your body triggers. You know.

Many of my clients think this work is one and done. They feel they have failed when they need to revisit their vision and goals. This could not be further from the truth. Your vision and goals are your compass. You lead the whole of your life when you check that compass not just daily, but choice by choice. This is the ultimate mindful living that will transform your experience of your whole life.

One of my mentors, Susanne Conrad, in her work at Lightyear Leadership provides brilliant tools for systematic vision and goal setting from clarity for your life and freedom from your past.

# BEGIN AGAIN: LESSON 6

You are never far from being the driver of your life. You've done great work over these three weeks, and these tools are always here for you.

We've been conditioned by our global culture to believe we can't guide our lives. That is a big fat lie that will keep you numb and constricted. At any moment *you realize* that you've given over your mental space to your job or your family, or to stress and fear, you have entered the domain of choice.

Noticing when you step out of your commitments to yourself, feeling tossed around like the bottle on the sea, you have just put mindfulness in action. With compassion and gratitude, you simply begin again. Revisit your commitments. Do your daily mindfulness practice. Reset healthy boundaries. Do your wellness work.

More than anything, stop judging yourself for falling off the wagon. As my teacher Susanne Conrad says, "Learn to fail fast." When you do, you can begin again faster, with more love, play, and delight.

You deserve to stop judging yourself and to start living powerfully. And I promise, the world will be a better place as you do.

How do you fail fast? Guess what? I'm not going to give you a process or practice. Everything you've already done in this book has laid the foundation. You simply begin again—begin your mindfulness practice again, begin living from your commitments again, begin making powerful requests again. You already have the tools. The difference is that when you get stuck or when something takes you out, you get back on track faster. This is the inner strength of compassion and kindness. It's yours to return to whenever you need.

# CULTIVATE WELL-BEING WITH LAUGHTER AND KINDNESS

There is nothing better for your well-being than laughter. It can strengthen your immune system, boost your mood, and diminish how you experience physical pain. This week, the goal is to spark some joy and laughter with your daily de-stress practice.

Joy, laughter, and happiness are not turning away from our challenges and suffering. They exist alongside the struggles of life. More importantly, laughter, delight, and joy are the endurance-builders you need for life. We could get into the science of it, and there is plenty to tell us that you get real physical benefits from laughter and play, but it's more important to do it.

When we feel exhausted, uncertain, or in a difficult place, it can be hard to even imagine laughing. We also have a cultural bias that the conditions of life should just dish up laughter without us having to try. This is partly because we think we need a reason to laugh, or that something should naturally cause our laughter. When this doesn't happen, we often take it as evidence that something is wrong with us or our lives.

Here's the cool thing: you don't need a reason to laugh, and you can seek out and even create laughter. When I'm battling a deadline, my mind tells me there is no time for fun. And yet many of us seem to find ways to avoid our work with mind-numbing (and I say "soul-deadening") internet or social media scrolling to "decompress."

What if when you get up to eat, or when you stop for the night, you pause and seek out laughter for even one minute? Especially if you don't feel like laughing, this can have profound effects on releasing stress from your body and lifting your spirits.

How do I suggest you seek out laughter? Here are a few great ways to bring some laughter into your day:

- Try a laughing meditation. I've included two different videos: the first takes you in slowly, the second drops you into the deep end. Both are great. You *will* feel absurd. And if you stick with it for a moment, it will likely at least get you to smile and chuckle, and that is enough.
    - o  Laughter Meditation for Beginners with Jagat Singh Bisht (https://youtu.be/p9jJNhDUQOk)
    - o  Just Laughing: A Mindfulness Meditation with Stephanie Nash (https://youtu.be/dDRr8UEIP9E)
- If you live with another person, expressly say, "I need to have a tickle war." Ask, and do, and see what happens. Kids are great for this.
- Seek out silly YouTubers who make you laugh. We go through cycles in our house of silly things that make us smile and giggle.
- Have a dance party—virtually, if needed. Get your friends together. Make a playlist that makes you happy, and dance, even for one song. You can also do this alone.

# Reflect and Choose

A s with previous weeks, set aside a few minutes to reflect. This simple pause helps you feel in control of your life. It's not a chore, rather a gift you give of commitment to yourself.

Here are a few questions you may find useful:

1. Did you have any insights about commitment and nonattachment?

2. What do you sense your life can feel and look like when you lead from commitment rather than reaction? Get specific about the body sensations and what you see.

3. What can you put in place to help you begin again when you find you've gotten off a path that you had chosen?

# CLOSE ONE WINDOW AND OPEN ANOTHER

As I noted in the beginning, the tools you started to play with in this book are "right now" and "always" tools. I've found that I travel through these tools over a few weeks and then go back and begin again. Some of them stay constant for me, like my daily mindfulness practice, revisiting my commitments each day, and gratitude. Others I pull out as I need them, such as self-compassion and setting healthy boundaries.

And sometimes I need this whole process. The beauty is that you know what you need when, and because you continue to listen for your body's sensations to guide you, you step forward with more ease and far less stress, always ready to begin again and again.

Trust that your winters will be followed by springs, and that your springs will bloom into summers. While eternal summer sounds delightful, we need autumn to harvest and the winter to regenerate and renew. You need not judge yourself or beat yourself for walking through uncertain and difficult times. These winters are your depth, and new life springs forth from these times.

Your mindful emerging is just that: you, emerging into a new life that you choose.

# Enjoy Being Guided

This entire program exists as an e-course with thirty-six videos to guide you through all of this work. Use code "ReadersSave30" to save $30 off the e-course. Find it here: https://badasshappyhuman. thinkific.com/courses/emerge-mindfully.

# ACKNOWLEDGEMENTS

The wisdom in this book has come together in this form because of the wise teachers who have come before me, and who so graciously share their light to illuminate the path for others. Nothing I have said here is incredibly new or unique. It's simply packaged in a way that I have found it personally useful and seen it make a difference for others.

This book draws heavily on work developed by Susanne Conrad, founder and creator of Lightyear Leadership. I would also like to acknowledge Tuere Sala, a guiding teacher at Seattle Insight Meditation. Her work with me in a previously very difficult year of my life allowed me to turn the straw of these last few years into gold for myself, the teams I lead, and the clients I coach. Thank you also to the countless teachers who have led me in retreats, programs, and through books. May your light shine through this book to serve others.